SIMPLY GREAT BREADS

SIMPLY GREAT BREADS

Sweet and Savory Yeasted Treats
from America's Premier Artisan Baker

Daniel Leader
with Lauren Chattman

PHOTOGRAPHY BY DITTE ISAGER

The Taunton Press

The Taunton Press
Inspiration for hands-on living®

The Taunton Press, Inc., 63 South Main Street,
PO Box 5506, Newtown, CT 06470-5506
e-mail: tp@taunton.com

Editor: Erica Sanders-Foege
Copy editor: Valerie Cimino
Indexer: Heidi Blough
Jacket & interior design: Carol Singer
Layout: Sandra Mahlstedt
Photographer: Ditte Isager
Food stylist: Simon Andrews
Prop stylist: Kim Ficaro

The following names/manufacturers appearing in
Simply Great Breads are trademarks:
All-Clad®, Bazzini®, Borough Market®, Bread Alone®,
Callebaut®, Chef's Warehouse®, Cooking.com®,
Ess-A-Bagel®, Ghirardelli®, Giusto's Vita-Grain Flours®,
Goldtouch™, Greenmarket®, H&H Bagels®, Henckels®,
King Arthur®, KitchenAid®, Maldon®, Marcato®, Nutella®,
Nuts Online®, Parker House®, Penzeys Spices®, Plugrá®,
SAF®, SaltWorks®, Scharffen Berger®, Toll House®,
Valrhona®, Viking®, Williams-Sonoma®, Wüsthof®

LIBRARY OF CONGRESS CATALOGING-IN-PUBLICATION DATA

Leader, Daniel.
 Simply great breads : sweet and savory yeasted treats
from America's premier artisan baker / Daniel Leader
with Lauren Chattman ; photographer, Ditte Isager.
     p. cm.
  ISBN 978-1-60085-297-8
 1. Bread. I. Chattman, Lauren. II. Title.
TX769.L376 2011
641.8'15--dc22

                    2010045866

For my dear parents, Faye and Bennett Leader, with love

ACKNOWLEDGMENTS

MY SINCERE THANKS to the following people for their tireless and ongoing efforts in making this book a success: Angela Miller, for taking care of the business details so that I could get baking; Lauren Chattman, for writing up my recipes and ideas; Sharon Burns-Leader, for developing and testing, retesting, and re-retesting every recipe until it was foolproof, and for working so hard to bake the breads in these photos; Octavia Fleck, for her invaluable part in the testing process; Simon Andrews, a wonderfully skilled food stylist and fun person to have at a photo shoot; Clare Fountain, part of the Bread Alone team who generously lent her talents to this project during the shoot; Ditte Isager, whose ability to bring out the beauty in every bread amazed me; photo assistant Ryan Liebe, for his tireless attention to detail in helping Ditte; prop stylist Kim Ficaro, for her impeccable taste; Alison Wilkes, for once again overseeing the design of a beautiful book; Valerie Cimino, for copy-editing the recipes and text to perfection; design manager Carol Singer and Sandra Mahlstedt, for seeing the book through the design and layout process; intern Heather Roussi, for taking care of so many important details; Sue Roman, Sharon Zagata, Catherine Levy, and Janel Noblin at Taunton Press, for their kindness and support; and, finally, Senior Editor Erica Sanders-Foege, for her thoughtful input at every step, from our first brainstorming meeting through editing and beyond. Her commitment and enthusiasm are inspiring.

CONTENTS

Introduction: Baking It Easy 2
....

CHAPTER 1

CLASSIC BREAKFAST BREADS 22

• "Luxury" English Muffins 26
• Crumpets 30
• Brioche Muffins 33

  VARIATIONS:
  • Fig Brioche Muffins 36
  • Chestnut Brioche Muffins 36
  • Cinnamon-Cardamom Brioche Muffins 36

• Quick Chestnut Cinnamon Sugar Spirals 37

  VARIATIONS:
  • Quick Cocoa-Mascarpone Spirals 40
  • Quick Apricot–Chocolate Chip Spirals 40

• Boiceville Bialys 41
• Authentic Bagels 45

CHAPTER 2

AN IDEAL BREAD BASKET 48

• Lightly Shaped Parker House Rolls 51
• Angel Biscuits 54
• Ham-and-Cheese-Filled Crescent Rolls 58
• Crisp Bread Sticks 60

  VARIATION:
  • Extra-Crisp Bread Sticks 62

• *Ciabatta* Rolls 63

  VARIATIONS:
  • *Ciabatta* with Bran 65
  • Seven-Seed *Ciabatta* Rolls 65

• Grilled Savory or Sweet *Ciabatta* 66
• Navajo Fry Bread 68

  VARIATION:
  • Chili-Dusted Navajo Fry Bread 70

• Whole Wheat Challah with Apricots 71

  VARIATION:
  • Whole Wheat Challah with Green Olives 73

CONTENTS

·······································

continued

CHAPTER 3

FLAVOR-PACKED FLATBREADS 74

• Pizza Dough for Grilling 78

  VARIATION:
  • Pizza Dough with Honey and Wine 80

• Grape *Schiacciata* 82

  VARIATIONS:
  • Rosemary-Walnut *Schiacciata* 84
  • Cherry Tomato–Anise *Schiacciata* 84

• Savory Yeasted Tart with Onion Confit
  and Olives 86
• *Mana'eesh* 89

  VARIATION:
  • *Mana'eesh* with Baked Eggs 92

CHAPTER 4

QUICK YEASTED TREATS 96

• Yeasted Pancakes 99
• Yeast-Raised Waffles 101

  VARIATION:
  • Whole Wheat and Flax Seed Yeasted
    Waffles 102

• Jelly-Filled Berliners 103

• Cider Doughnuts 108

   VARIATION:
   • Glazed Cider Doughnuts 110

• Banana Doughnuts with Maple-Walnut Glaze 111
• Stone Fruit Beignets 114
• Fontina *Bombolini* 117
• Yeasted Coffee Cake with Simple Almond
  Topping 121

   VARIATION:
   • Yeasted Coffee Cake with Fancy Pecan
     Topping 122

• Chocolate Babka 123
• Caramel Monkey Bread 127

   VARIATION:
   • Garlic and Scallion Monkey Bread 130
....

Equivalency Charts 132
Glossary of Baking Terms 133
Resources 134
Index 135

INTRODUCTION

BAKING IT EASY

DURING MY CAREER as a professional baker and cookbook author, I've traveled the world in search of techniques and recipes for delicious handcrafted breads. Like other artisan bakers of my generation, I fell in love, years ago, with sourdough loaves built in two or more stages and raised with natural starters instead of commercial yeast. I've adapted recipes for French *levain* baguettes, German sourdough ryes,

and sunny yellow Italian semolina sourdough rounds so that I could make them at my bakery in the Catskills. I've written extensively about sourdough techniques and European sourdough traditions in my books, *Bread Alone* and *Local Breads*.

When I first decided to open a European-style bakery in upstate New York, there wasn't a book written in English on what I needed to know in order to make my first loaf. So I traveled to Paris and apprenticed myself to a French baker. But I wasn't alone for long in baking and writing about this type of bread.

Since *Bread Alone* was published in 1993, dozens of knowledgeable books on artisan bread have been published. Now passionate home bakers eager to learn about and commit themselves to baking sourdough and other kinds of long-fermenting breads can go to the library or Amazon.com and easily find a recipe for a Poilâne-style *miche* or a German *graubrot*. It is an embarrassment of riches and a wonderful validation of my belief in the importance of preserving and promoting old bread ways.

A lot of ink has been spilled on the subject of bread because there is so much fascinating history, culture, science, and technique informing our craft. These days, it is not a lack of information that prevents home bakers from trying their hand at making bread in the traditional ways. It is often simply a question of finding the time. Although there is nothing particularly difficult about cultivating natural yeast and using it to raise bread, it can't be done on the spur of the moment. Indeed, as I am reminded every time I visit my bakery, Bread Alone®, in the middle of the night to check on my starters, artisan bread crafting with sourdough and other long-fermenting starters is a lifestyle choice! To bake a loaf of sourdough bread, you first have to cultivate a wild yeast starter, which can take a week or longer. You have to feed and care for your starter on schedule and bake with it regularly to maintain its rising powers. Making sourdough bread is generally not a onetime thing. Starter maintenance and bread baking get added to the daily or weekly routine of kitchen tasks and household chores: a joy for some, but too burdensome for others to attempt.

Although I have an abiding love of well-crafted sourdough breads, I have always been curious about and open to enjoying yeasted breads and pastries that are decidedly simpler to make. In my previous books, I was careful to include some recipes employing commercial yeast, for beginners and others not ready to go full-out artisan. I am perfectly comfortable with and very proud of these recipes, for *pain ordinaire*, *Bavarian pretzels*, *pizza alla Romana*, and a few others. After all, these are traditional European-style breads with just as much history and integrity as the world-famous *pain Poilâne*.

Many of my readers have baked their way through the recipes made with commercial yeast and then hit a wall. I've received countless letters and e-mails from these bakers, asking, "Is this as far as I can go without venturing into sourdough territory?"

"Hardly!" I want to reply. I have a large reservoir of absolutely delicious recipes, both classic and unusual, using commercial yeast and mostly mixed in one step. For a long time now, I have wanted to share some of them with readers who have enjoyed the simpler recipes in my previous books and are hungry for more. This new collection, including a chocolate babka my grandmother would be proud of, a beautiful Alsatian onion and olive tart, and the tallest English muffins you've ever seen, is for all of you.

SIMPLE BAKING WITH INTEGRITY

Because I am a fan of simple yeasted baked goods like Parker House® rolls, crisp Italian bread sticks, and tender jelly doughnuts, I am often dismayed by the treatment they get in "easy" or "simple" baking books. While artisan baking books focus on techniques and ingredients for unlocking the flavor of wheat and other grains, books promising quick and simple breads often load on the yeast, sugar, and fat, which in large quantities don't serve grains but instead mask their flavor. When I taste a bagel, I want to experience a clean wheaty flavor balanced with its characteristic chewy texture. I don't want the sugar and yeast to jump out at me first. When I bite into a jelly doughnut, I expect a delicately crisp and greaseless crust yielding to a light interior with just a hint of sweetness, surrounding a small and absolutely delicious spoonful of the best-quality fruit preserves.

There needn't be such a great divide between "artisan" bread recipes and quick ones. In fact, by taking the same kind of care with ingredients and technique, a home baker can certainly make a roll, bread stick, or doughnut worthy of the artisan label. To wind up with the lightest and most well-risen little breads, gently round your Parker House rolls instead of brutally flattening and folding the dough. Get out your pasta machine to cut your bread sticks in the same way that bakers in Italy have cut bread sticks for generations. Reduce your apple cider on top of the stove before adding it to your dough for the most intensely flavored cider doughnuts you've ever tasted.

Well-made bread doesn't have to come from a recipe that resembles a scientific treatise.

While artisan bread recipes can run for several pages, the recipes in this book are not much longer or more difficult to follow than the recipe for Toll House® cookies. Take a look at the recipe for Yeasted Pancakes on page 99. It is not one bit more complicated than a standard pancake recipe with baking powder. But using yeast in the batter gives you pancakes that are ethereal in their bubbly lightness, quite in contrast to the often doughy and heavy pancakes made with baking powder. Baking with yeast does take some planning—it is difficult to make a yeasted bread or pastry in less than a few hours from start to finish. But, as you'll see when you make the Grape *Schiacciata* on page 82 (which requires about 15 minutes of active work and about 2½ hours to rise and bake), you don't have to invest weeks or days in the process to wind up with something very satisfying indeed.

To get such results, craft your simple breads and yeast-raised treats with the same sensitivity and attention to detail that you would use for an artisan loaf. If you choose the best ingredients, handle them properly, and learn to understand your dough as it develops, then you are approaching the process as an artisan. You are on the fast track to making a bagel, bread stick, or jelly doughnut that's as good to eat in its own right as any true artisan bread.

DETAILS, DETAILS

In baking, little things can make a big difference in the quality of your bread. Individual recipes will give relevant tips for getting the best results, but here are a few general suggestions for making the simple breads and yeasted pastries in this book as good as they can be.

GO ORGANIC

When I first started baking, I had to search far and wide for organic ingredients. Now, organic flour, cornmeal, seeds, nuts, eggs, milk, and butter are available at natural foods stores and most supermarkets. Not only do organic ingredients make better-tasting breads and pastries, but they also have a gentler impact on our environment. Yes, they cost more. But compared to the price of a loaf of bread you'd buy from your local bakery, a homemade organic loaf is still a bargain.

WEIGH YOUR INGREDIENTS

In my bakery, I follow the same procedures every time I bake. I weigh my ingredients on a scale, make sure they're all at the same temperature, and use a timer so that every batch of dough is kneaded, fermented, proofed, and baked to the same degree. It is more difficult to be so consistent at home, and you'll inevitably have to make adjustments from time to time: The temperature of your kitchen will be cooler in the winter than in the summer, so you'll have to alter your schedule accordingly. Flour's ability to absorb water varies from season to season and brand to brand, so you might have to add more or less water to your dough. But without question there is one thing you can do to get the same great bread consistently: Invest in a digital scale and always measure your ingredients by weight instead of by volume. Measuring by volume is simply not as reliable. Depending upon how much your flour has settled in the bag, 1 cup may weigh between 135 and 145 grams. That difference will result in two distinctly different breads.

JUST ADD WATER

Rustic Italian breads such as pizza and *ciabatta* traditionally contain a high proportion of water, which gives them a moist, bubbly crumb. But many other doughs benefit from high hydration, a fact that I took into consideration when developing a range of recipes, not just the ones for Italian flatbreads. So if your bialy dough seems wet as you knead it, just go with it for a while, resisting the impulse to add extra flour. This is easier to accomplish with an electric mixer and a dough hook than it is by hand, so when a dough is particularly wet, I recommend pulling out a KitchenAid® mixer.

GIVE KNEADING A REST

As dough is kneaded, the proteins in the flour organize themselves into a stretchy web, called *gluten*, that will expand along with the gases that are a by-product of yeast and will solidify in the oven (like the steel skeleton of a skyscraper), providing the finished bread with its crumb structure. Large, chewy artisan breads often require lengthy kneading to develop a strong gluten structure that can support a high rise. But many of the items in this book are small, tender, and/or flat. This means that they don't require as much gluten as larger, crusty, high-rising breads. In fact, too much kneading can overheat your dough, leading to over-fermentation. Even when a bubbly crumb is desired, as with *ciabatta*, it can be achieved by kneading minimally and then giving the dough a turn.

USE THE MIXER LIKE AN ARTISAN

There is nothing like hand kneading to teach you about your dough. When you have contact with dough from start to finish, you can actually feel the gluten organizing itself as the dough is transformed from a lumpy, bumpy mass into a smooth and coherent one. But there is no doubt that using a powerful standing mixer with a dough hook will save you time and is often a better choice than hand kneading, especially if you are an inexperienced hand kneader and/or are working with a very wet dough. Most of the recipes in this book call for machine kneading, for ease and speed. Just make sure, when kneading with a mixer, to stop every so often to touch the dough. Press it, stretch it, run your fingers over it, just as you would when hand kneading. Frequent contact with the dough will teach you to recognize when it is properly kneaded.

KEEP THINGS COOL

The recipes in this book, in contrast to what old-fashioned American baking manuals usually direct, call for room temperature water and room temperature fermentation. Lowering the traditional temperature in this way will cause your dough to rise more slowly, which is a good thing, since a long, slow fermentation allows flavor to build in the dough. Remember, there is absolutely no work involved in letting your dough sit on the countertop to reap this benefit. Quite a few recipes in this book direct you to place your dough in the refrigerator for several hours or overnight. Refrigeration slows fermentation down, allowing you some flexibility in deciding when to bake, and builds incredible flavor without the risk of over-fermentation.

TRY A PRE-FERMENT

If you want a small taste of what a sourdough starter does for bread, try a recipe that employs a pre-ferment, which instantly "ages" a dough to which it is added, giving it flavor that it otherwise wouldn't have time to develop during its relatively short fermentation period. Using a simpler (than sourdough) two-stage method for making dough, you just mix a small quantity of flour, water, and yeast and let it begin to ferment before adding it to a larger quantity of dough that you make later. A pre-ferment can give simple breads such as *ciabatta* surprisingly complex flavor.

DEVELOP YOUR PROOFING SKILLS
Judging when to put the challah, brioche, or Parker House rolls into the oven is one of the biggest challenges an inexperienced baker faces. Under-proofed breads will have a tight, undeveloped crumb. Over-proofed doughs will lose volume when they go into the oven and lose flavor because of excess gas. In general, properly proofed breads will look pillowy but not over-inflated.

PREHEAT YOUR BAKING STONE
This simple step makes a big difference. When raw dough hits hot stone, the internal combustion creates a nicely risen dough. Using a baking stone improves the rise and enhances the crust color and flavor on items you might not have thought of as hearth breads, such as bagels or Parker House rolls.

PICK A RECIPE AND PERFECT IT
Is your dad famous for his incredibly fluffy cheese omelet or your Aunt Sally known for her crisp-on-the-outside, moist-on-the-inside savory veal meatballs? If so, it is because practice makes perfect. Practice is especially important when working with yeast doughs, which become friendlier the more you get to know them. The first time you make Angel Biscuits (page 54), you won't know exactly how long to knead the dough so that it's sticky but coherent. You'll have to guess how to cut the dough decisively but without tearing or stretching it. The second time you make them, you'll have a previous experience for comparison. By the fifth time, you will be well on your way to becoming famous for your tender biscuits.

THE BIG FOUR
Even the world's greatest breads consist of just a few ingredients: the most gently processed grain, the purest water, the most active instant yeast, and the most flavorful sea salt. High-quality ingredients, properly handled, will produce the best-tasting baked goods.

WHEAT FLOUR
The flour you use will determine the flavor and texture characteristics of your bread, so choose carefully. Flour is milled from wheat

berries, which consist of three parts: the starchy endosperm, the germ (the berry's embryo, from which new grain can sprout), and the tough outer husk, or bran. Whole wheat flour consists of whole berries that have been ground to a fine powder. White flour is sifted to remove the germ and the bran. If you are buying whole wheat flour, look for grain that has been stone-ground at a smaller mill rather than put through rollers at a larger commercial mill. Stone milling preserves the enzymes in the wheat berries, and enzymes are good for fermentation.

Before white flour is ready to be sold, it must be aged to bring out its gluten-forming capabilities. If you are buying white flour, look for a brand that is unbleached and unbromated, which means it is has been naturally aged by being stored for several weeks, during which time it develops its gluten-forming potential simply by coming into contact with oxygen in the air. Chemically treating flour with bleach or bromate is a way to hasten the aging process. But bleach destroys the natural beta-carotene pigment in flour, which subtly colors and flavors bread. And bromate, a gluten-maximizing additive, is outlawed throughout Europe as a carcinogen.

The protein content of the flour you choose will affect the texture of your bread. The more protein a flour contains, the more gluten it can form when kneaded with water. Most of the recipes in this book use unbleached all-purpose flour, which has between 10 percent and 12 percent protein, producing well-structured loaves that are still soft enough to chew.

Again, I highly recommend seeking out organic flour at your local natural foods store or from one of several reputable online sources (see Resources on page 134). The bottom line: Organic flour makes better-tasting bread.

WATER

When it comes to water, the choice is a question of taste. Most tap water is just fine in bread dough. If your tap water tastes good enough to drink, then go ahead and use it when you bake. If it is so full of minerals or chlorine that you drink bottled spring water, then use bottled spring water when you bake. A moderate mineral content is good for bread dough, so stay away from distilled water, which contains no minerals at all.

YEAST

I call for instant yeast in these recipes because it is the most convenient and commonly available to home bakers. Unlike traditional active dry yeast, which needs to be rehydrated in water or another liquid before being mixed into bread dough, instant yeast can be combined with flour before any water is added. It will become fully hydrated during kneading. Any brand of yeast will work in these recipes, but I

prefer SAF® yeast (see Resources on page 134) for its liveliness and reliability.

If you'd like to substitute active dry yeast for instant yeast, it is easy to do so. Just moisten it in water for a few minutes (or whatever liquid is called for in the recipe) before combining it with the flour and other dry ingredients.

Definitely avoid rapid-rise yeast, so called because it has been packaged with yeast foods and enzymes to accelerate fermentation. This type of yeast will cause your dough to ferment so quickly that it won't have any time at all to develop flavor. In addition, there is a real risk of over-fermentation when using rapid-rise yeast, the result being a loaf that collapses in the oven.

FINE SEA SALT

I prefer the pure taste of sea salt in my breads. Or I'll sometimes use unadulterated kosher salt. Iodized table salt tastes flat in comparison. When I bake at home, I use *fleur de sel*, imported from France. But there are many wonderful-tasting sea salts now available (see Resources on page 134).

EVERYTHING ELSE

Quite a few breads in this book get great flavor and texture from additional ingredients. As when choosing the big four, select any add-ins with quality and flavor in mind.

BUTTER

The recipes in this book call for unsalted butter. Salt in butter can mask off flavors and, in any case, will make your dough too salty. European-style butters such as Plugrá® will make a super-rich brioche, but any good supermarket brand will work.

BUTTERMILK

Buttermilk adds tangy flavor to a variety of easy breads. It keeps for several weeks in the refrigerator, so if you use a small amount to make Angel Biscuits (page 54), save the rest for Yeasted Pancakes (page 99) or Yeast-Raised Waffles (page 101).

CHEESE

High-quality Parmesan, cheddar, and mascarpone add richness and flavor to some of the breads in this book. Artisanal breads require artisanal cheese, so buy high-quality cheese such as aged Italian Parmesan, farmhouse Vermont cheddar, and imported Italian mascarpone from a reputable source for best results.

CHOCOLATE

Only the best bittersweet chocolate will do for the Chocolate Babka on page 123. Choose either a good European brand like Valrhona® or Callebaut® or a high-quality domestic brand such as Scharffen Berger® or Ghirardelli®.

CORNMEAL

Cornmeal adds color, flavor, and crunch to "Luxury" English Muffins (page 26). Buy stone-ground yellow meal, which contains plenty of flavorful and healthy corn oil, and store it in an airtight container in the refrigerator or freezer to keep it fresh for months.

DRIED FRUIT

Look for organic unsulfured dried fruits at your natural foods store or online (see Resources on page 134). Soak dried fruits in water so that they plump up and don't absorb water from the dough.

EGGS

Eggs are packaged according to weight, so for the sake of consistency all of the recipes in this book call for large (2-ounce) eggs. White or brown makes no difference, although do try to buy organic eggs.

MALT POWDER

If you want to make authentic bagels, sweeten your dough the way they do at H&H Bagels® in New York City, with non-diastatic malt powder, derived from barley.

MILK

I used organic whole milk to test these recipes. You may substitute 2 percent milk, but I don't recommend low-fat or skim milk, which may be too lean to give you the best flavor and texture.

NUTS AND SEEDS

Nuts and seeds contain flavorful oils that enrich a variety of breads. I buy organic nuts and seeds in bulk (see Resources on page 134) and store them in zipper-lock bags in my freezer. If directed, toast nuts before adding them to dough, to bring out their full flavor.

OLIVE OIL

Use a fruity and aromatic olive oil in recipes where olive oil is needed. Even a small amount of best-quality extra-virgin olive oil will give bread a beautiful aroma and silky texture.

VEGETABLE OIL

To fry doughnuts, beignets, and Navajo fry bread, I use flavorless canola oil or vegetable oil.

EQUIPMENT FOR EASY BAKING

For thousands of years, people made bread with virtually no equipment at all beyond a surface for mixing and kneading dough, a cloth for covering it as it fermented, and a wood-fired oven. The *Mana'eesh* on page 89 were originally baked on hot stones over an

open fire! You can certainly still take the minimalist approach when outfitting your kitchen, but a few key pieces of modern equipment (most of them inexpensive and easy to find) will make your baking life easier and improve the quality of many of your breads. Pick and choose from the following items depending on your ambitions, your budget, and how much time you have to produce handmade bagels, yeasted coffee cake, and focaccia.

Baker's Peel This long-handled, rimless sheet comes in handy for sliding breads onto a preheated baking stone. If you don't have one, use a rimless baking sheet.

Baking Sheets Choose heavy-duty stainless steel baking sheets, which conduct heat well. Avoid dark-colored sheets, which can scorch the bottoms of rolls and bread sticks. Avoid nonstick baking sheets for the same reason, and also because nonstick coating will be damaged at the very high heat required to bake some breads. It's good to have both rimless and rimmed sheets, the latter coming in handy for doughs that get their shape from the bottom and sides of the sheet, such as Grape *Schiacciata* (page 82).

Baking Stone There is no better way to get a professional artisan effect at home than by baking your bread on a stone. A preheated baking stone conducts heat directly to the bottom of your loaves, mimicking the heat of a professional hearth oven. Baking stones are relatively inexpensive (a large one costs less than $50) and with proper care will last forever. Choose the largest baking stone that your oven can accommodate (the better to bake two dozen bagels or a large focaccia) and make sure it is at least ½ inch thick, since thinner stones tend to crack. Be sure to season your new stone by heating it once or twice in a moderately hot oven, following the manufacturer's instructions, so that it won't break the first time it is heated to your oven's highest setting.

Bench Scraper A rectangular steel blade with a wooden handle on one of the long edges, a bench scraper cuts cleanly through dough that needs to be divided. Alternatively, use a sharp chef's knife.

Cake Pan I've found that Goldtouch™ pans from Williams-Sonoma® (see Resources on page 134) release even the stickiest cakes and breads, like the Caramel Monkey Bread on page 127.

Cast-Iron Pan A cast-iron pan, which conducts heat beautifully, is a good choice for griddled flatbreads and pancakes. I also use mine to create steam in my oven, by preheating the cast-iron pan on the lower rack while preheating the baking stone and then dropping water or ice cubes into it when loading my breads into the oven. (Steam prevents the exterior of the bread crust from drying out before the interior has finished expanding and thus allows the bread to reach its full potential rise.)

Dough-Rising Container If you put your dough into a straight-sided clear container, it is easy to judge how much it has increased in volume. Premarked containers with lids in various sizes are available through King Arthur® (see Resources on page 134).

Dough Scraper A soft and flexible plastic tool that bakers use to scrape dough out of bowls, a dough scraper has a rounded, beveled edge that fits any size bowl and cleanly removes even the stickiest dough from a bowl. Use a rubber spatula (it won't be quite as neat) if you don't have a dough scraper.

Electronic Digital Scale Invest in a high-quality electronic digital scale for weighing your ingredients. When you use one, your baking will become more consistent. Buy a scale that will show the weight of your ingredients in ounces and grams. I prefer to weigh my ingredients in grams (the recipes in this book give weights in both ounces and grams) for the sake of precision. And try to buy a scale with a tare function, so you can zero out the scale before adding the next ingredient to your bowl.

English Muffin Rings and Cake Rings These stainless steel rings keep English muffin dough in shape and contain flowing crumpet batter (see Resources on page 134).

Heavy-Duty Standing Mixer The doughs in this book can be mixed and kneaded very successfully in a heavy-duty standing mixer with a dough hook (handheld mixers and lightweight mixers with metal beaters are not powerful enough to knead bread dough). I used the smallest KitchenAid standing mixer, the K45SS (see Resources on page 134), to test the recipes and was quite happy with the results. Adding too much flour during hand kneading will make your breads tough and dry, but using a standing mixer will help you avoid this common pitfall, so you can knead your moist dough without being tempted to add extra flour.

Loaf Pan If you've ever made a banana bread, you already own this inexpensive pan. Use it to make Chocolate Babka (page 123) or Whole Wheat Challah with Apricots (page 71). If you are in the market for a new pan, buy one with a nonstick finish.

Measuring Cups and Spoons If you don't have a scale, you can measure your ingredients by volume, with cups and spoons. Be sure to use dry-measure metal or plastic cups for dry ingredients. Use the "dip and sweep" method, scooping up your flour from the bag or canister and then leveling off the excess with a knife or metal spatula. Use glass liquid measuring cups for water and other liquids, gauging the accuracy of your measurement by looking at the cup at eye level. Small measuring spoons are fine for measuring salt and instant yeast, but again, be sure to level the ingredients with a knife or spatula before adding them to the mixture.

Mixing Bowls A set of nesting stainless steel mixing bowls, available at any cookware shop or online (see Resources on page 134), will help you organize and mix your bread ingredients.

Muffin Tin If you have a 12-cup standard-size muffin tin, you'll be able to make the beautiful Brioche Muffins on page 33.

Parchment Paper I use parchment paper to line the baker's peel or rimless baking sheet before placing loaves on top for the final rise. This way, I can slide the shaped dough, still on the parchment, right onto the baking stone without worrying that it will stick to the peel and possibly deflate during the transfer.

Pastry Brush Use a pastry brush—preferably one with silicone bristles, which don't shed—to give your Whole Wheat Challah with Apricots (page 71) or Brioche Muffins (page 33) a coat of egg wash. Dry pastry brushes are also good for brushing excess flour from the surface of a shaped loaf.

Pizza Cutter Not only is this sharp wheel good for cutting just-baked pizza, but it can also cut rolled dough for bread sticks and other flat items cleanly and quickly.

Plastic Wrap Prevent your fermenting dough from drying out by covering the bowl with a sheet of plastic wrap. Later, during proofing, lightly drape floured or oiled loaves with plastic wrap for the same reason.

Rolling Pin You'll need a rolling pin to roll out the dough for Quick Chestnut Cinnamon Sugar Spirals (page 37), as well as a few other recipes. Use whatever kind of pin you are comfortable with: tapered or straight, with or without handles. All will work.

Rubber Spatula Before kneading your dough by hand or with the standing mixer fitted with the dough hook, it's a good idea to give all of the ingredients a few turns with a rubber spatula to moisten the flour.

Pasta Machine I have a Marcato® Atlas hand-crank pasta machine, which I use to make bread sticks (see Resources on page 134).

Serrated Knife I count my high-quality bread knife as an essential tool. It allows me to slice my breads cleanly, without tearing them and destroying their crust and crumb. Invest in a hand-forged serrated knife from a respected manufacturer. (I like Wüsthof®, Henkels®, and Viking®.)

Stockpot or Large Dutch Oven You will need a large, deep pot for poaching bagels and frying doughnuts.

Thermometers An instant-read thermometer will let you take the temperature of your water and other bread ingredients, so you can see if they are in the fermentation-friendly range of 70°F to 78°F. You can also use it to take the internal temperature of a bread to help you judge its doneness. In general, a crusty, rustic bread like *Ciabatta* Rolls (page 63) should be baked to an internal temperature of 205°F, while a softer enriched bread, like Chocolate Babka (page 123), should be baked to 190°F. It is also a good idea to hang an oven thermometer from the rack in your oven to check its temperature. Some ovens run hot and some run cold, and if yours runs either way you'll need to adjust either the oven temperature or the baking time for best results.

Waffle Iron A heavy-duty waffle iron, such as one from All-Clad® (see Resources on page 134), will give you wonderfully crisp waffles.

Wire Cooling Rack Cool your breads on a wire rack so that air can circulate underneath them, allowing their undersides to become crisp instead of soggy.

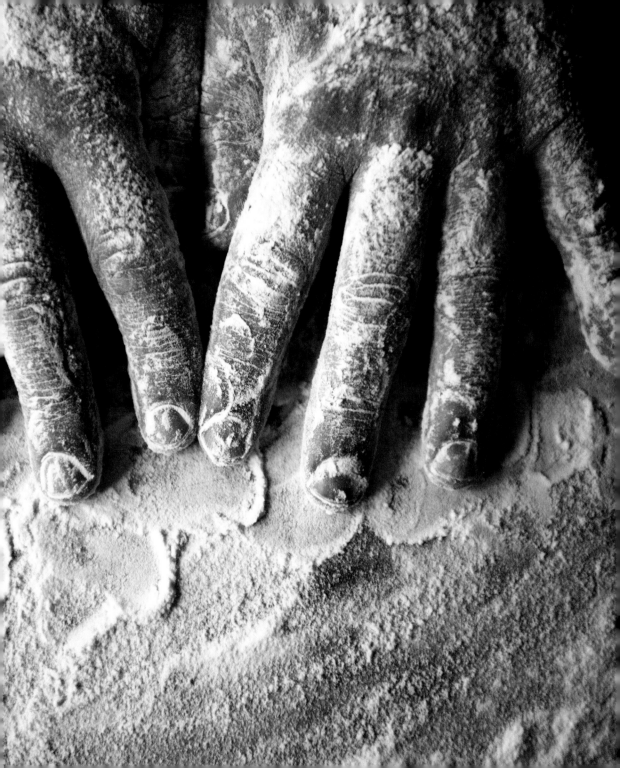

CLASSIC
BREAKFAST BREADS

IN THE PAST 10 YEARS, an abundance of books on artisan baking have been published, making recipes for baguettes, Poilâne-style *miche*, and *pane Pugliese* available to every home baker. Excellent examples of these and many other European artisan breads are increasingly common in bakeries, gourmet stores, and even supermarkets across the country. When it comes to European artisan breads, we have an embarrassment of riches.

But books on artisan baking generally favor large crusty loaves at the expense of classic small breads like bagels and English muffins. At the same time, these classic small loaves are becoming more and more difficult to find in bakeries. Rubbery commercial examples abound in every coffee shop and convenience store, but unless you live near H&H Bagels on the Upper West Side of New York City or near the Flour Station in London's Borough Market®, it's difficult to find a handcrafted old-fashioned bagel or English muffin anymore.

The recipes in this chapter are designed to fill the gap in the serious home baker's repertoire with thoughtful recipes for a few delicious breakfast items that are easy to make at home. These are breads that have always given me an inordinate amount of pleasure. Of course, I want readers to experience the same sense of ease and enjoyment that I get when making them for myself and my family. But I also feel a real sense of urgency. Great bialys are increasingly difficult to find at the shop around the corner. If you want to experience the pleasure of eating them, you had better learn to make them yourself.

As with any artisan bread, success is in the details. Making an excellent English muffin requires as much attention to ingredients and technique as does making an excellent baguette. This isn't to say that the process must be difficult or complicated. In fact, the longer I bake bread the more I recognize that simpler is often better when it comes to getting great results. There's no need to cultivate a sourdough starter to make the ultimate English muffin, although sourdough fanatics will argue otherwise. Instead, use buttermilk to give your muffins a creamy tartness. Make them extra tall so that there's more of the fluffy interior to enjoy, and start them on the griddle and finish them off in the oven so they bake through. Buy the freshest stone-ground cornmeal to give the crust on your muffins delicious crunch and golden color.

For the bubbliest crumpets, use both yeast and baking soda, taking care to add just the right amount of water to encourage the formation of large butter-catching nooks and crannies on the surface of each one. Beyond this, time your baking carefully. Crumpets are best when eaten straight from the pan.

I've been making brioche loaves at my bakery for years, so I know very well that using bread flour and adding butter to the partially kneaded dough in small increments is the best way to encourage a high rise in the oven. When I'm at home, I prefer to bake this dough in muffin tins, the better to enjoy a larger proportion of flavorful crust per serving!

As a kid growing up in Buffalo, I went crazy for the bags of bagels and bialys that my grandfather would buy at Mastman's Kosher Delicatessen to bring to our house on weekends. Good bagels and bialys evoke in me a deep nostalgia for the days when this type of honest bread was available and even taken for granted in every Jewish neighborhood. To reexperience this childhood pleasure at my home in the Catskills, I make my own. You can, too. Use malt powder, like I do, for authentic sweetness. Or substitute some sugar if it's more convenient. Just don't skip the step that separates true bagels from cheap imitations, the brief dip in boiling water that sets their shiny crusts and gives them their dense, slightly spongy interiors.

And learn, as I did when I spent a morning at Kossar's Bialys on Grand Street in New York City, how to shape a traditional bialy, pricking the center with a fork so it doesn't bubble up during baking, and filling it with a rich spoonful of sautéed onions mixed with poppy seeds.

"LUXURY" ENGLISH MUFFINS

This recipe was inspired by the English muffins I saw on a visit to London's Borough Market. Unlike the inch-thick, pallid packaged specimens I was familiar with from my local supermarket and diner, these were a good 2 to 3 inches tall, with a beautiful golden brown griddled crust.

I knew that it would take a few tricks to bake these extra-tall muffins successfully, but the result was well worth the effort. They start on the griddle, in baking rings, to keep them in shape (if you don't have rings, you can fashion some from cleaned tuna cans, removing the top and bottom lids and smoothing out any metal burrs before using them—a tip I learned years ago from the classic cookbook *Laurel's Kitchen*). Because they are so thick, they won't cook all the way through on the griddle, as do conventional English muffins, so they must be finished off in the oven. The trickiest thing about this recipe is keeping track of your muffins as they bake. First, they need to be browned on both sides—don't skimp on the butter, which gives the crust such great flavor—and cooked enough so that they won't collapse when handled. As soon as they are browned, they must be transferred to the preheated oven to bake through. Don't become so involved with browning the next batch that you forget to remove the first batch from the oven as soon as they are done!

For those iconic nooks and crannies, insert the tines of a fork into the middle of the muffins all the way around, and then pull apart before slathering with butter and jam.

17.64 ounces/500 grams (3½ cups) unbleached bread flour

.44 ounce/13 grams (3¼ teaspoons) sugar

.24 ounce/7.5 grams (1½ teaspoons) fine sea salt or kosher salt

.25 ounce/7 grams (1¾ teaspoons) instant yeast

12 ounces/350 grams (1½ cups) room temperature buttermilk (70°F to 78°F)

Cornmeal, for dusting

1 ounce/28 grams (2 tablespoons) unsalted butter

1. Combine the flour, sugar, salt, and yeast together in a large mixing bowl or the bowl of a standing mixer fitted with the dough hook. Add the buttermilk and stir with a rubber spatula or mix on medium speed until a rough dough comes together.

2. Knead the dough until it is smooth, 8 to 10 minutes on medium-low speed. It will be a fairly stiff dough. Cover the bowl with plastic wrap and let stand at room temperature until it doubles in size, 1 to 1½ hours.

3. Grease a baking sheet and then dust it with cornmeal. Turn the dough onto a floured countertop and divide it into 10 equal pieces. Round each piece into a ball (see "Instructions for Shaping Rounds" on page 44) and place the balls on the prepared baking sheet. Sprinkle the tops of the dough balls with more cornmeal and cover loosely with plastic wrap. Let stand at room temperature until puffy and almost doubled in size, 1 to 1½ hours.

4. Preheat the oven to 350°F. Place a clean baking sheet in the oven. Heat a cast-iron griddle or skillet on top of the stove over medium-low heat.

5. Melt a teaspoon or two of the butter on the preheated griddle. Coat your baking rings with butter and place as many as will fit on the hot griddle. Gently place a ball of dough into each ring on the heated griddle and cook until the bottoms are well-browned, 8 to 10 minutes. Carefully flip each muffin in its ring and cook until golden on the other side. Take care not to turn the English muffins too soon. You want to wait until they are well set, or they might collapse.

6. As the muffins are browned, place them on the baking sheet in the oven and bake until they are cooked through, 6 to 8 minutes. Transfer the fully baked muffins to a wire rack as they are cooked through.

7. Repeat with the remaining muffins, adding more butter to the pan as needed and transferring the griddled muffins to the oven to finish baking. Let the muffins cool completely on the rack before serving. "Luxury" English Muffins are best eaten on the day they are made. For longer storage, freeze in a zipper-lock plastic bag for up to 1 month. To defrost, place on the countertop for 15 to 30 minutes, and reheat in the oven at 350°F for 5 minutes before serving.

INSPIRATION FOR THE BAKER:
LAUREL'S KITCHEN

The recipes in this book are filled with ideas and flavors and techniques that I've borrowed from my mentors. But I developed these recipes in my home kitchen, to please my family and myself, and I'd like to acknowledge the influence of a cookbook author beloved by many home bakers of a certain age, Laurel Robertson, in shaping my thinking about items like English muffins and crumpets many years ago.

The idea for using old tuna cans instead of baking rings first appeared in *Laurel's Kitchen*. More than a collection of vegetarian recipes, *Laurel's Kitchen* is a guide to living as close to the land as is feasible, being creative as a craftsperson in the kitchen, and making the best nutritional decisions for your family and community. The bread section takes up very little of the book, but it has the elegance and intelligence of a private journal, and it includes simple explanations and no-nonsense ideas (such as baking bread dough in juice cans instead of loaf pans) that still appeal to the homebody in me. When I first read the book in 1976, its impassioned insistence on the importance of living artfully electrified me, and it continues to inspire me today:

"Why compartmentalize our lives so that art is a thing apart? There is an artistic way to carry out even the simplest task, and there is a great fulfillment to be had from finding out that way and perfecting it. That is the silent message that comes to us in the village handicrafts we value so. A culture that gives priority to speed and greed and multiplicity—well, it is no culture, it has no culture. To lead lives of artistry, we have only to slow down, to simplify, to start making wise choices."

—Laurel's Kitchen, *Nilgiri Press*

CRUMPETS

Like many Americans, I always assumed that crumpets were close relatives of English muffins (an assumption that apparently infuriates the British!). When I tasted my first crumpet at the Crumpet Shop in Seattle, I was blown away. It was a little bit spongy and had beautiful holes on top, perfect for absorbing farm-fresh butter and local honey. They were so delicious that it's a shame there's not a Crumpet Shop on every corner. But there's a reason why most bakeries shy away from making crumpets. They're best when made to order. If they sit around for even a couple of hours, to me they won't have the same just-griddled goodness.

At that moment, I knew I wanted to develop a yeasted crumpet recipe of my own. It thought it would be so much fun to stand around the kitchen with friends and family on a rainy day and serve them hot from the griddle, with cups of steaming tea. The result more than lived up to my fantasy. Try them. If you are like me, you will always remember where you had your first crumpet!

6.11 ounces/173 grams (1⅔ cups) unbleached all-purpose flour

8.04 ounces/228 grams (2 cups) unbleached bread flour

.07 ounce/2 grams (¾ teaspoon) cream of tartar

.56 ounce/17 grams (1 tablespoon plus ½ teaspoon) fine sea salt or kosher salt

15.63 ounces/443 grams (2 cups) room temperature water (70°F to 78°F), plus more if necessary

.22 ounce/7 grams (2¼ teaspoons) instant yeast

.06 ounce/2 grams (½ teaspoon) sugar

.06 ounce/2 grams (½ teaspoon) baking soda

4.78 ounces/136 grams (⅔ cup) room temperature milk (70°F to 78°F)

Unsalted butter, for greasing the cake rings

1. Place the all-purpose flour, bread flour, cream of tartar, and salt in the bowl of a standing mixer fitted with the paddle attachment. Stir to combine.

2. Whisk together the water, yeast, and sugar in a medium bowl and let stand until foamy, about 10 minutes.

3. Pour the water mixture into the flour mixture and mix on low speed to combine. Cover the bowl with plastic wrap and let stand at room temperature for 1 to 1½ hours.

4. Dissolve the baking soda in the milk, and then pour the milk mixture into the bowl with the batter. Stir gently to combine. The batter should now be the consistency of pancake batter. If it's too stiff, your crumpets won't have enough of those characteristic bubbles and holes, so, if necessary, add more water, a tablespoon at a time, to reach the right consistency.

5. Heat a large nonstick skillet over medium-low heat. Grease several 4-inch cake rings with butter.

6. Place the cake rings in the skillet and pour some batter into each ring so they're three-quarters full. Cook until holes begin to form on the surface, 7 to 8 minutes. Remove the rings, flip the crumpets, and cook for another 2 to 3 minutes, until nicely toasted. Serve immediately with butter. For longer storage, freeze in a zipper-lock plastic bag for up to 1 month. To defrost, place on the countertop for 15 to 30 minutes, and reheat in the oven at 350°F for 5 minutes before serving.

BRIOCHE MUFFINS

I've been making classic brioche at my bakery, Bread Alone, for many years. It's just one of those happy, wonderful foods that never disappoints. Every time I treat myself to a fresh slice, with a cup of strong coffee, I get as much pleasure as I did when I first discovered this bread.

You'll notice that I call for bread flour and may wonder why, if the goal is to bake a soft and yielding bread. Brioche is rich in fat from the butter and eggs. During mixing, the fat molecules coat the proteins in the flour, inhibiting the formation of gluten that the bread needs to give it a strong structure to support a high rise. To make sure that enough gluten develops, in spite of all of the added fat, you need to use flour with a higher gluten content. Don't worry. Your brioche will be exceptionally tender.

Shaping brioche in the traditional way requires a special technique and pan. To get a similar effect without the work or the equipment, you can roll the dough into small balls and place the balls in a conventional muffin tin, three per cavity. The result is brioche muffins that are beautiful and fun to pull apart as you eat them. I like to sprinkle pearl sugar (see Resources on page 134) over the muffins just before baking, but you can use sanding sugar or leave them plain and they will be just as good.

This recipe makes just the right amount of dough for a 9-inch loaf. Shape it as you would any pan loaf (see "Pan Loaf Shaping Instructions" on page 40), place it in a greased 9-inch loaf pan, and bake it for 40 to 45 minutes at 425°F. Leftovers make sensational French toast, especially when served with local apples and pears cooked with some butter and brown sugar.

17.63 ounces/500 grams (3½ cups) unbleached bread flour

2.12 ounces/60 grams (⅓ cup) sugar

.48 ounce/15 grams (1 tablespoon) instant yeast

.24 ounce/7.5 grams (1½ teaspoons) fine sea salt or kosher salt

6 large eggs

2 ounces/48 grams (¼ cup) chilled water (55°F)

10 ounces/140 grams (2¼ sticks) unsalted butter

2 tablespoons pearl sugar (optional)

1. Combine the flour, sugar, yeast, and salt in the bowl of a standing mixer. Combine 5 of the eggs and the water in a bowl or glass measuring cup. Cut the butter into ¼-inch pieces. Place all of the ingredients in the refrigerator until well-chilled, about 2 hours.

2. Add the egg and water mixture to the bowl with the flour. Stir a few times with a rubber spatula until a rough dough forms. Fit the mixer with the dough hook and knead on medium speed until the dough is smooth and some gluten has developed, 5 to 6 minutes.

3. With the mixer running, add the butter, 1 piece at a time. Do this rhythmically, without waiting for all of the previous butter to be incorporated. When you've added all the butter, the dough will be a lumpy mess. Keep kneading it in the mixer until it comes back together and is smooth, shiny, and cohesive, 4 to 5 minutes.

4. Scrape down the dough hook and the sides of the bowl with a spatula, cover the bowl with plastic wrap, and let stand at room temperature for 1 hour. Then refrigerate overnight, 8 to 12 hours.

5. Spray a 12-cup muffin tin with nonstick cooking spray. Divide the dough into 12 equal pieces. Divide each piece into 3 equal pieces and quickly roll the pieces into small balls. Place 3 balls into each of the muffin cups (the dough will fill the cups). Sprinkle the muffins lightly with flour, drape with plastic, and let rise until doubled in volume, 1½ to 2 hours.

6. One hour before baking, place a baking stone on the middle rack of the oven. Preheat the oven to 375°F.

7. Lightly beat the remaining egg and brush the muffins with it. Sprinkle them with the pearl sugar, if desired. Bake until golden brown, 20 to 25 minutes, tenting them with aluminum foil after 15 minutes or so if they are browning too quickly.

8. Transfer the muffin tin to a wire rack and let stand for 10 minutes before inverting the muffins onto the rack, re-inverting them, and letting them cool completely. Brioche Muffins will keep at room temperature in an airtight container for up to 2 days. For longer storage, freeze in a zipper-lock plastic bag for up to 1 month. To defrost, place on the countertop for an hour or two, and reheat in the oven at 350°F for 5 minutes before serving.

VARIATIONS

It's hard to imagine improving on plain brioche, but if you are looking for a change of pace, here are some fantastic variations that rival the original recipe.

FIG BRIOCHE MUFFINS

Add 3 stemmed and finely chopped moist dried figs to the dough after you've added half of the butter.

CHESTNUT BRIOCHE MUFFINS

Add 1 ounce/28 grams of chestnut purée (see Resources on page 134) to the dough along with the flour.

CINNAMON-CARDAMOM BRIOCHE MUFFINS

Add 1 teaspoon of cinnamon and ¼ teaspoon of cardamom to the dough along with the flour.

QUICK CHESTNUT CINNAMON SUGAR SPIRALS

Shaping brioche into the classic *tête* is a little tricky. It takes some practice to form the topknot that sits on top of the larger dough round in the traditional fluted brioche pan in such a way that it doesn't look lopsided and sloppy. If you don't have time to practice your technique, here is another very simple slice-and-bake method for shaping brioche dough. Chestnut purée is available at specialty food stores and many supermarkets (look for it in the baking aisle). If you can't find it, try one of the variations that follow.

FOR THE FILLING

2 ounces/56 grams (4 tablespoons) unsalted butter, softened

7.76 ounces/220 grams (1½ cups) packed light brown sugar

.18 ounce/5 grams (1 teaspoon) ground cinnamon

.71 ounce/20 grams (2 tablespoons) chestnut purée

1 recipe dough for Brioche Muffins, prepared through step 4 (page 33)

FOR THE ICING

2.5 ounces/60 grams (½ cup) confectioners' sugar

4 ounces/100 grams (⅓ cup) heavy cream

1. **Make the filling:** Combine the butter, brown sugar, cinnamon, and chestnut purée in a medium bowl. Mix thoroughly and then set aside.

2. Roll the brioche dough into a ½-inch-thick rectangle measuring about 16 by 8 inches. Position the dough horizontally, with a long side closest to you. Spread the filling evenly over the dough. By hand, roll the dough up into a snug log from the long end. Pinch the outside edges to seal. Wrap the log tightly in plastic wrap and refrigerate for at least 1 hour and up to 12 hours. (Alternatively, you can freeze the dough log for up to 1 week and defrost it in the refrigerator for 2 hours before proceeding.)

3. Line a rimmed baking sheet with parchment paper or thoroughly butter a 12-cup muffin tin. Use a sharp chef's knife to cut the log into 12 equal pieces and place them, cut side up, on the sheet or in the cups of the tin. Drape the dough pieces with plastic wrap and let rise at room temperature until doubled in size, 1 to 1½ hours.

4. Preheat the oven to 375°F. Uncover the dough pieces and place the baking sheet or muffin tin in the oven. Bake for 30 minutes, rotate the pan, and continue to bake until golden, 35 to 40 minutes longer.

5. **Make the icing:** While the spirals are baking, whisk the confectioners' sugar together with ¼ cup heavy cream, adding more as necessary, until the glaze is thick and smooth but pourable.

6. Remove the spirals from the oven. Slide them, still on the parchment, onto a wire rack. If they are in a muffin tin, remove them from the muffin tin immediately, using a thin metal spatula, so that they don't stick to the pan. Let them cool for 20 minutes on the rack. Place the rack over a platter or baking sheet and drizzle the spirals with the glaze. Let the glaze harden (this will take about 30 minutes), and then serve immediately. Quick Chestnut Cinnamon Sugar Spirals will keep at room temperature in an airtight container for up to 2 days. For longer storage, freeze in a zipper-lock plastic bag for up to 1 month. To defrost, place on the countertop for an hour or two, and reheat in the oven at 350°F for 5 minutes before serving.

VARIATIONS

QUICK COCOA-MASCARPONE SPIRALS

Replace the chestnut filling with this mixture for a delicious variation on the main recipe.

4 ounces/100 grams (¼ cup) currants or raisins

2 ounces/52 grams (1 tablespoon) dark rum

3.53 ounces/100 grams (½ cup) sugar

.18 ounce/5 grams (1 teaspoon) unsweetened cocoa powder

4 ounces/100 grams (¼ cup) mascarpone cheese

1. Combine the currants and rum in a small bowl and let stand at room temperature for at least 1 hour and up to 12 hours.

2. Whisk together the sugar and cocoa powder in a small bowl.

3. Spread the mascarpone evenly over the rolled dough. Drain the currants and scatter them over the dough. Sprinkle the sugar mixture over the currants. Roll, let rise, and bake as directed.

QUICK APRICOT–CHOCOLATE CHIP SPIRALS

Here's an even quicker way to fill your brioche dough to make spirals.

4 ounces/100 grams (¼ cup) apricot jam

7.21 ounces/200 grams (1 cup) semisweet chocolate chips

Stir the apricot jam until it is smooth. Spread the jam evenly over the rolled dough. Sprinkle with the chocolate chips. Roll, let rise, and bake as directed.

PAN LOAF SHAPING INSTRUCTIONS

Follow these steps for the most delicious and gorgeous results when shaping pan loaves.

1. To fit dough into a loaf pan, shape it into a round, let it stand on the counter to rest for 5 minutes, and then flatten it into a rectangle about an inch shorter than your loaf pan.

2. Position the dough horizontally, with the longer edge facing you, and fold the rectangle over lengthwise (to create a cylinder), and then gently roll it back and forth on the counter until it is the same length as the pan.

3. Place the loaf, seam side down, into the pan and gently press on it so that it is touching the pan on all sides.

BOICEVILLE BIALYS

I spend a lot of time in New York City, selling bread at the Union Square Greenmarket®. Whenever I can, I make the trip a little farther downtown to the Lower East Side. First, I'll stop at the Doughnut Plant at 379 Grand Street for one of the incredible yeasted doughnuts, and then I'll move a few doors down, to 367, where Kossar's Bialys has been producing superior bialys, bagels, bulkas, pletzels, and other kosher bread specialties for more than 65 years.

I enjoy watching Kossar's bakers expertly pull each *tagelach* (the Yiddish word for "dough ball") into the characteristic shape before filling all their indented centers with fresh onions and poppy seeds. Our production schedule at Bread Alone has never allowed me to make bialys, but this hasn't stopped me from making them at home, attempting every time to achieve the same lightness and flavor that they achieve at Kossar's. My recipe is pretty faithful to the original. The bialys come out light and bubbly, with a thin but wonderfully crisp crust. When you make them, don't forget to prick the indented centers with a fork. If you don't, they will bubble up.

If you want to serve these for breakfast, you can make the dough the night before, let it rise, and then refrigerate the shaped dough balls. While the oven heats the next morning, make the filling and make the wells in the balls. Bake and serve warm, with smoked salmon. (I eat my Boiceville Bialys with locally smoked salmon from the Catskill Artisan Smokehouse in nearby Wallkill; see Resources on page 134.)

FOR THE FILLING

2 teaspoons olive oil

1 medium onion, finely chopped (about 1 cup)

1 tablespoon poppy seeds

½ teaspoon fine sea salt or kosher salt

Ground black pepper, to taste

FOR THE DOUGH

12.16 ounces/345 grams (1½ cups) room temperature water (70°F to 78°F)

1 package (.25 ounce/7.5 grams/ 2¼ teaspoons) instant yeast

17.63 ounces/500 grams (4 cups) unbleached all-purpose flour

.24 ounce/7.5 grams (1½ teaspoons) fine sea salt or kosher salt

1. **Make the filling:** Heat the olive oil in a medium skillet over medium heat. Add the onion, poppy seeds, salt, and black pepper. Cook, stirring occasionally, until the onion is translucent but hasn't yet started to color, 5 to 7 minutes. Set aside to cool completely.

2. **Make the dough:** Pour the water into the bowl of a standing mixer. Add the yeast, flour, and salt and stir with a rubber spatula just until all the water is absorbed and a rough dough forms. Attach the dough hook and knead the dough on medium speed until it is springy and smooth, 5 to 6 minutes.

3. Transfer the dough to a lightly oiled bowl or dough-rising container, cover the bowl with plastic wrap, and let stand at room temperature until it has doubled in volume, about 2 hours.

4. Line a baker's peel or a rimless baking sheet with parchment paper. Set another piece of parchment paper on the counter. Turn the dough out onto the parchment paper on the counter and use a bench scraper or sharp chef's knife to divide it into 10 equal pieces. Shape each piece into a tight round (see "Instructions for Shaping Rounds" on page 44).

5. Transfer half of the rounds, seam sides down, to the lined peel or baking sheet, leaving at least 2 inches between each one. Transfer the other half to the other piece of parchment paper. Lightly dust with flour, drape with plastic wrap, and let stand until increased in size about 1½ times, about 1½ hours.

6. One hour before baking, place a baking stone on the middle rack of the oven. Preheat the oven to 450°F.

7. Press both thumbs into the center of each bialy, creating a shallow well. Don't make the center too thin—think about making a mini pizza. Pierce the wells with the tines of a fork to prevent them from bubbling up in the oven. When all of the bialys are shaped, fill each one with a heaping teaspoon of the filling.

8. Slide the first batch of bialys, the ones on the peel or baking sheet, onto the baking stone. Bake until golden brown, 7 to 9 minutes.

9. Slide the peel or the rimless baking sheet under the parchment paper to remove the bialys from the oven. Cool for about 5 minutes on a wire rack, and then peel them off the parchment paper. Repeat with the second batch of bialys, sliding them, still on the

parchment, onto the peel or baking sheet, and then sliding them, still on the parchment, onto the baking stone. Bialys are best eaten on the day they are baked. For longer storage, freeze in a zipper-lock plastic bag for up to 1 month. To defrost, place on the countertop for 15 to 30 minutes, and reheat in the oven at 350°F for 5 minutes before serving.

INSTRUCTIONS FOR SHAPING ROUNDS

Many of the breads in this book have unique shapes (such as bagels, brioche spirals, and crumpets). When this is the case, I include specific shaping instructions in the recipe. But I turn to a very basic technique when getting quite a few other breads ready for the oven: rounding the dough. Dough for items as different from each other as "Luxury" English Muffins (page 26), Navajo Fry Bread (page 68), and Fontina *Bombolini* (page 117) all begin to shape up as rounds. Here is the basic technique.

1. Collect the dough into a rough ball.

2. Cup one or two hands (depending on the size of the ball—one hand will be sufficient for small items like bombolini; if you are shaping challah dough into a large round, you will need to use two hands).

3. Use your cupped hand or hands to rotate the dough in tight circles as you move it toward you on the countertop. These two simultaneous motions will pull any rough bits underneath the ball, creating a taut surface.

AUTHENTIC BAGELS

Ten years ago you couldn't walk a few blocks in New York City without stumbling upon a good bagel place. But times have changed, and today it is difficult to find a real bagel, one that has been boiled before it's been baked. There are a handful of well-established bagel bakeries in New York that make bagels by shaping them on boards and then dropping them into giant steam kettles to set and gelatinize the crusts before loading them into the oven. Most of the bagels you see today are simply baked, using a lot of steam in the hopes that this extra moisture will take the place of actual boiling.

So, to get an authentic bagel you'll probably have to make it yourself. For the most flavorful bagels, take a few tricks from a professional baker's bag. The perfect bagel has a wonderfully balanced flavor, sweet but also a little tangy. To accomplish this, prepare a pre-ferment to add some tangy flavor to the dough, which will balance the sweetness of the malt powder, a traditional bagel sweetener (see Resources on page 134). But don't *not* make bagels if you can't find malt powder. You can substitute the same amount of brown sugar or dark honey. To give your bagels that shiny golden crust, boil them in water to which you've added some malt syrup (or sugar or molasses) and baking soda. The malt syrup and baking soda will help to caramelize it, giving it good color and flavor.

For seeded bagels, drain the poached bagels briefly on a clean kitchen towel and then roll them in a shallow bowl filled with seeds before transferring them to a baking sheet for baking.

FOR THE PRE-FERMENT

10 ounces/283 grams (1¼ cups) room temperature water (70°F to 78°F)

8.8 ounces/250 grams (1¾ cups plus 1 tablespoon) unbleached bread flour

.06 ounce/2 grams (½ teaspoon) instant yeast

FOR THE DOUGH

.05 ounce/1.5 grams (½ teaspoon) instant yeast

6.88 ounces/195 grams (1¾ cups plus 1 tablespoon) unbleached bread flour

.18 ounce/5 grams (1 teaspoon) malt powder

.11 ounce/3 grams (¾ teaspoon) fine sea salt or kosher salt

1.7 ounces/49 grams (2 tablespoons plus 2 teaspoons) baking soda

.3 ounce/10 grams (1 tablespoon) sugar, molasses, or malt syrup

1 ounce/28 grams (¼ cup) sesame or poppy seeds (optional)

1. **Make the pre-ferment:** Combine the water, flour, and yeast in the bowl of a standing mixer. Whisk until smooth, scraping down the sides of a bowl with a spatula when you are done. The mixture will resemble pancake batter. Cover with plastic wrap and let stand at room temperature until bubbly and foamy, about 2 hours.

2. **Make the dough:** Add the yeast to the pre-ferment and stir thoroughly. Add the flour, malt powder, and salt and knead on medium-low speed using a dough hook until the dough is elastic and smooth, about 10 minutes.

3. Transfer the dough to a lightly oiled bowl or dough-rising container, cover the bowl with plastic wrap, and let stand at room temperature for 1 hour. The dough won't rise much but will be easier to handle after a rest.

4. Line a baking sheet with a piece of parchment paper and sprinkle with flour. Turn the dough out onto a lightly floured countertop and use a bench scraper or sharp chef's knife to divide it into 8 equal pieces. Lightly shape each piece into a round.

5. Begin creating your bagels by gently stretching a hole into the center of the dough rounds with your thumbs, using gentle pressure. Don't worry if your bagels look uneven. During boiling, this unevenness will disappear. Place the shaped bagels on the floured parchment paper. Drape the bagels with plastic wrap and refrigerate for at least 6 hours or overnight.

6. One hour before baking, place a baking stone on the middle rack of the oven. Preheat the oven to 500°F.

7. Bring a large pot of water to a boil. Line a baker's peel or rimless baking sheet with a fresh sheet of parchment paper and spray with nonstick cooking spray. Spread a clean kitchen towel on the counter.

8. Add the baking soda and sugar to the boiling water and stir to dissolve. Use a skimmer to transfer the bagels one by one to the boiling water. Don't overcrowd them; just cook 3 or 4 at a time. Boil, turning once, until their surfaces are shiny and beginning to harden, about 1 minute on each side. Remove them from the water and transfer to the towel to drain. If desired, have a dish with a layer of sesame or poppy seeds nearby. Dip the tops of the bagels in the seeds to coat.

9. Working quickly (don't let the bagels sit for more than 2 minutes on the towel), transfer the bagels to the parchment paper and slide the bagels, still on the parchment, onto the baking stone. Bake until golden brown, 10 to 14 minutes.

10. Slide the peel or rimless baking sheet under the parchment paper to remove the bagels from the oven. Cool for about 5 minutes on a wire rack, and then peel them off the parchment paper. Bagels are best eaten on the day they are baked. For longer storage, freeze in a zipper-lock plastic bag for up to 1 month. To defrost, place on the countertop for 15 to 30 minutes, and reheat in the oven at 350°F for 5 minutes before serving.

AN IDEAL
BREAD BASKET

HAVE YOU NOTICED, when you go to a restaurant, that the bread basket on your table always holds slices of baguette or country bread, but it almost never includes old-time classics like Parker House or crescent rolls? That's probably because good country bread is easy for chefs to buy, while good Parker House rolls (not the flabby commercial product sold alongside sliced white bread at supermarkets) can't be bought at any price.

In my house, dinner without fresh and delicious bread is unthinkable. But sometimes, instead of bringing home a loaf from work, I enjoy serving buttery little rolls, crunchy bread sticks, and chewy individual *ciabatta* rolls that I can only get from my home oven. In this chapter, I've collected the recipes for breads I include in my ideal home bread basket.

What makes it ideal? A variety of textures and flavors—soft, crisp, salty, savory, buttery, lean. I love the idea of picking at different breads, without filling up, as I enjoy a glass of wine and a salad before bringing out the main course. Each bread has to be excellent in its own right and a little bit different from the next.

My Lightly Shaped Parker House Rolls (page 51) don't have the traditional shape, for a reason. I love this dough, but noticed that when I over-handled it during shaping I got a denser and less well-risen bread. Gently rounding the dough instead resulted in a lofty rise and light texture that made me very happy.

To my baker's palate, Angel Biscuits (page 54)—biscuits made with yeast as well as baking powder—have a more complex and interesting flavor than biscuits raised with baking powder only. While baking powder biscuits become stale quickly, Angel Biscuits taste fresh for longer than a few minutes out of the oven, and they freeze beautifully.

Real Italian bread sticks are a special passion of mine. I love to use my pasta machine the way Italian bakers use a special bread stick machine to shape them at home. I make dozens at a time. If I'm not going to eat them all within several days, I'll make an extra-crisp variation, baking the bread sticks until they are very dry and cracker-like, so that they'll stay fresh for several weeks.

Armed with these recipes and a few others, an ideal bread basket is not just a fantasy. With a little forethought, you can easily assemble one at almost a moment's notice. Every time you bake a batch of rolls, set some aside to freeze in a zipper-lock bag. Every time you'd like to put together an ideal bread basket, pull one or two of each from the freezer, defrost on the countertop, and warm them in the oven at 350°F for 5 minutes. Add a few bread sticks and your ideal bread basket has materialized in time for dinner, any night of the week.

LIGHTLY SHAPED
PARKER HOUSE ROLLS

Conventional Parker House rolls are made with a straight dough (a dough that is mixed in a single stage). I like to add a pre-ferment, a small portion of dough that is made ahead of time and mixed into a larger batch later. A pre-ferment contributes a layer of fermented flavor to the rolls and helps me divide the preparation time into manageable segments. For Sunday dinner, I mix the pre-ferment in the late morning, while enjoying a cup of coffee. After a short hike or some gardening, I finish the dough and set it aside to ferment. In the late afternoon, I shape the rolls, let them rest, and, later, bake them, just as the steaks are ready for the barbecue.

I'm less concerned with giving these rolls a traditional shape (in which you flatten and fold over the dough) than with handling the dough as lightly as possible to preserve its gluten structure. I simply cut the buttery dough into pieces and gently round them. This minimal shaping results in a higher-rising roll with a wonderfully light texture.

I always keep my baking stone in my home oven, so I don't forget to preheat it when I'm baking bread. I've had some tasty surprises as a result. Cooked on a baking sheet on top of the stone, my roasted vegetables are always beautifully caramelized. When I put a pot of beef stew directly on the stone, the sauce is darker and deeper than when I place the pot on a rack. When I first made Parker House rolls, I placed the pan on the preheated stone and was very pleased with the results. They were crusty and delicious. You can always bake them on the oven rack if you don't have a baking stone. They'll still be delicious, if not quite so puffy and browned.

FOR THE PRE-FERMENT

5.16 ounces/146 grams (1 cup) unbleached all-purpose flour

5.68 ounces/161 grams (¾ cup) room temperature water (70°F to 78°F)

.62 ounces/18 grams (1 tablespoon) honey

.01 ounce/.75 gram (¼ teaspoon) instant yeast

FOR THE DOUGH

12.87 ounces/365 grams (2⅓ cups) unbleached all-purpose flour

1.27 ounces/36 grams (¼ cup) room temperature milk (70°F to 78°F)

.1 ounce/3 grams (1 teaspoon) instant yeast

5.28 ounces/150 grams (1⅓ sticks) unsalted butter, softened

.16 ounce/5 grams (1 teaspoon) fine sea salt or kosher salt

1. **Make the pre-ferment:** Combine the flour, water, honey, and yeast in the bowl of a standing mixer. Use the paddle attachment to mix until smooth. Cover the bowl with plastic wrap and let stand for 1 to 4 hours at room temperature, or overnight in the refrigerator.

2. **Make the dough:** Add the flour, milk, yeast, butter, and salt to the bowl with the pre-ferment. Give the mixture a few turns with a rubber spatula to moisten all of the ingredients, and then mix on medium-low speed with the dough hook until it is shiny and smooth, 8 to 10 minutes.

3. Transfer the dough to a lightly oiled bowl or dough-rising container, cover the bowl with plastic wrap, and let stand at room temperature until it has doubled in volume, 1½ to 2 hours.

4. One hour before baking, place a baking stone on the middle rack of the oven. Preheat the oven to 400°F. (If you are not using a baking stone, preheat the oven 15 to 20 minutes before baking.) Lightly butter a baking sheet.

5. Turn the dough out onto a lightly floured countertop and use a sharp chef's knife or bench scraper to divide into 2 equal pieces.

6. Lightly shape each one into a log. Cut each log into 12 equal pieces. Cover the pieces with plastic wrap so they don't dry out. Then, 1 piece at a time, lightly round each one (see "Instructions for Shaping Rounds" on page 44).

7. Place the lightly rounded rolls on the prepared baking sheet in even rows, leaving at least 1 inch between each roll. Butter a piece of plastic wrap and drape it loosely over the rolls. This is a little messy, but it will make the rolls tasty and prevent sticking. Let the rolls rise until puffy, about 1½ hours.

8. Uncover the baking sheet and place the pan directly on the baking stone, if you are using one. Bake until the rolls are nicely browned, 18 to 20 minutes. Transfer them to a wire rack to cool. Serve warm or at room temperature. Lightly Shaped Parker House Rolls are best eaten on the day they're baked. Freeze uneaten rolls in a zipper-lock plastic bag and reheat in the oven at 350°F for 5 minutes before serving.

ANGEL BISCUITS

Baking powder biscuits are great, but the addition of yeast to the formula elevates them to a different level entirely. I'm biased, of course, but I love the slightly fermented flavor that you add to biscuits when you rest the dough in the refrigerator overnight. The crust is also improved, crispier, and more caramelized because of this fermentation.

Angel Biscuits take some planning ahead but aren't any more difficult to make than baking powder biscuits. To achieve this new complexity with your biscuits, you only have to do about 5 minutes of work the evening before you want to eat them, and then let time do the rest. Use some cake flour for tenderness. And try baking them on a baking stone for the best oven spring.

10.58 ounces/300 grams (2½ cups) unbleached all-purpose flour

7.05 ounces/200 grams (1½ cups) cake flour

.35 ounce/10 grams (2¼ teaspoons) baking powder

4.41 ounces/125 grams (¾ cup) sugar

.25 ounce/7.5 grams (2½ teaspoons) instant yeast

.05 ounce/2 grams (¼ teaspoon) fine sea salt or kosher salt

10 ounces/140 grams (2¼ sticks) unsalted butter, cut into bits and frozen

12.35 ounces/350 grams (1½ cups) chilled heavy cream

1. Combine the all-purpose flour, cake flour, baking powder, sugar, yeast, and salt in the bowl of a standing mixer or a large mixing bowl. With the paddle attachment in place and the mixer on low speed, or with your fingertips, press the butter into the flour as you do when making pie dough, until the mixture resembles coarse, flaked meal. Do this quickly with your fingertips if using your hands, so that the butter won't melt.

2. With the mixer and paddle attachment on the lowest speed, or with a wooden spoon, stir in the cream until the mixture is moistened through. You will be able to form the dough into a ball, but it will be very soft and sticky.

3. Leave it in the bowl, cover with plastic wrap, set in a warm place, and let it rise until doubled, about 1½ hours.

4. Gently deflate the dough by pressing down on it with your hands, re-cover the bowl, and place it in the refrigerator for at least 4 hours or overnight.

5. If you are using a baking stone, place the stone on the middle rack of the oven and preheat for 1 hour before baking. Preheat the oven to 350°F. Line a baker's peel or rimless baking sheet with parchment paper.

6. Turn the dough onto a lightly floured countertop and pat to a thickness of about 1 inch. Using a 2½-inch biscuit cutter, cut out as many biscuits as you can, dipping the cutter in flour as you go to avoid pulling and tugging at the dough. As for the scraps, don't re-roll them or even push them together to form extra biscuits. Place the larger scraps on the sheet with the biscuits—they will make nice treats for the baker!

7. Place the pan in a warm place—near the preheating oven is good. Drape the biscuits with plastic wrap and let them rise until puffy and soft-looking, about 1 hour.

8. If you are using a baking stone, slide the biscuits, still on the parchment, onto the stone (alternatively, place the baking sheet on the middle rack of the oven) and bake them until they are lightly browned and cooked through, 10 to 15 minutes.

9. Slide the biscuits, still on the parchment, onto a wire rack to cool slightly. Serve warm. Angel Biscuits are best eaten on the day they're made. Freeze uneaten biscuits in a zipper-lock plastic bag for up to 1 week and reheat in the oven at 350°F for 10 minutes before serving.

SHRIMP SALAD

I love to split the Angel Biscuits and make small, delicate sandwiches with them. A lightly dressed shrimp salad is the perfect filling. The following recipe makes enough to fill 12 small sandwiches, a nice, light lunch for 4 people. For neater eating, serve the salad over butter lettuce leaves, with the biscuits on the side.

SHRIMP SALAD WITH AVOCADO AND PICKLED CACTUS

MAKES ABOUT I POUND

Look for pickled cactus (*nopalitos en escabeche*) on the shelf with the Mexican foods at your supermarket.

¼ cup extra-virgin olive oil

1 tablespoon freshly squeezed lime juice

2 tablespoons finely chopped fresh cilantro

1 pound small cooked shrimp, peeled and chopped

½ small ripe avocado, peeled, pitted, and diced

¼ cup finely chopped pickled cactus

Salt and ground black pepper, to taste

Whisk together the olive oil, lime juice, and cilantro in a large bowl. Add the shrimp, avocado, and pickled cactus, and toss to coat with the dressing. Season with salt and pepper. Serve inside or alongside Angel Biscuits.

HAM-AND-CHEESE-FILLED CRESCENT ROLLS

Cream cheese makes these rolls marvelously tender and gives them a slightly tangy flavor. The honey sweetened pre-ferment, a simple but important step, elevates these humble crescents without the bother of making a complex laminated dough (one that has alternating layers of dough and butter like that which is used to make croissants). Your guests will be amazed at these delicately formed, yet easy-to-make treats. You can make them without the ham and cheese, or use different fillings. I've used oven-dried toma-toes, roasted peppers, or slivered olives with some sliced almonds. I've also made sweet crescents filled with mini chocolate chips and raspberry or apricot jam. Cinnamon sugar on its own is good, too.

FOR THE PRE-FERMENT

5.16 ounces/146 grams (1 cup) unbleached all-purpose flour

5.68 ounces/161 grams (¾ cup) room temperature water (70°F to 78°F)

.62 ounce/18 grams (1 tablespoon) honey

.05 ounce/1 gram (¼ teaspoon) instant yeast

FOR THE DOUGH

12.67 ounces/365 grams (2⅓ cups) unbleached all-purpose flour

.13 ounce/4 grams (1 teaspoon) instant yeast

.26 ounce/7 grams (1 teaspoon) fine sea salt or kosher salt

1.27 ounces/36 grams (¼ cup) room temperature milk (70°F to 78°F)

1.93 ounces/55 grams (¼ cup) cream cheese, softened

3.5 ounces/70 grams (7 tablespoons) unsalted butter, softened

2 slices ham, each cut into 8 strips

2 slices Swiss cheese, each cut into 8 strips

1. **Make the pre-ferment:** Combine the flour, water, honey, and yeast in the bowl of a standing mixer. Mix with the paddle attachment until smooth, a minute or two. Cover the bowl with plastic wrap and let stand at room temperature for 1 to 4 hours, or refrigerate overnight.

2. **Make the dough:** Add the flour, yeast, salt, milk, cream cheese, and butter to the bowl with the pre-ferment and knead on low speed with the dough hook until the dough comes together in a ball. Turn the mixer to medium speed and continue to knead until the dough is smooth and shiny, 4 to 6 minutes more. Transfer the dough to a lightly oiled bowl or dough-rising container, cover the bowl with plastic wrap, and let stand at room temperature until it has doubled in volume, 1½ to 2 hours.

3. Grease 2 baking sheets with butter. Turn the dough out onto a lightly floured countertop and divide into 2 equal pieces. Lightly round each piece (see "Instructions for Shaping Rounds" on page 44).

4. Cover 1 dough round with plastic wrap to prevent it from drying out, and roll the other dough round into a 14-inch disk. With a pizza wheel or sharp paring knife, cut the disk into 8 wedges. Place a piece of ham and a piece of cheese near the widest part of each wedge. Starting with the wide edge, roll the dough into tight crescents and place on the prepared baking sheet, leaving 2 inches between crescents. Repeat with the remaining dough, ham, and cheese.

5. Butter some plastic wrap and drape it over the rolls. Let them stand at room temperature until puffy, about 1 hour.

6. One hour before baking, place a baking stone on the middle rack of the oven. Preheat the oven to 400°F.

7. Uncover 1 sheet and place it directly on the baking stone. Bake until the rolls are golden, about 20 minutes. Transfer the rolls to a wire rack to cool. Repeat with the remaining rolls. Serve warm or at room temperature. Ham-and-Cheese-Filled Crescent Rolls are best served on the day they're baked. Freeze uneaten biscuits in a zipper-lock bag for up to 1 week and reheat in the oven at 350°F for 10 minutes before serving.

CRISP BREAD STICKS

These are crisp and flavorful and a perfect addition to my ideal bread basket. And unlike other items that come out of my oven, these bread sticks will keep for a week in an airtight container at room temperature. This recipe has a high yield, so you can make them and have them around for a week or so, if they don't get eaten first. They are great, healthy snacks, they go well with soups and salads, and they can be served alongside any of the other rolls or biscuits in this chapter for an impressive but easy assortment at dinnertime.

In Italy, bakeries have special machines to shape these, similar to the machines that extrude pasta. At home, you can use a hand-crank pasta machine (see Resources on page 134) to get almost identical results. If you don't have a pasta machine, roll out the dough as thinly as you can, adding as little flour as you can, and cut it into long, thin pieces with a paring knife or pizza wheel.

Sprinkling the seeds (instead of cornmeal or flour) on the bottom of the baking sheet is a good way to prevent sticking while adding flavor and crunch.

8 ounces/240 grams (1 cup) room temperature water (70°F to 78°F)

17.64 ounces/500 grams (3½ cups) unbleached bread flour

.12 ounce/3.75 grams (1¼ teaspoons) instant yeast

.24 ounce/7.5 grams (1½ teaspoons) fine sea salt or kosher salt, plus more for sprinkling (optional)

1.5 ounces/60 grams (3 tablespoons) honey

1 ounce/35 grams (2 tablespoons) Worcestershire sauce

.3 ounce/10 grams (2¼ teaspoons) olive oil

Sesame seeds, for sprinkling

Poppy seeds, for sprinkling

1. Pour the water into the bowl of a standing mixer. Add the flour, yeast, salt, honey, Worcestershire sauce, and olive oil. Stir with a rubber spatula until a rough dough forms. Using a standing mixer fitted with a dough hook, knead the dough on medium speed until it is firm and supple and no longer tacky, about 5 minutes.

2. Transfer the dough to a lightly oiled bowl or dough-rising container, cover the bowl with plastic wrap, and let stand at room temperature until it has doubled in volume, about 1½ hours.

3. Place 2 oven racks in the top third and bottom third positions and preheat the oven to 375°F. Sprinkle the bottoms of 2 baking sheets with the sesame seeds or a combination of seeds and sea salt.

4. Cut the dough into 8 equal pieces. Cover all but 1 piece with plastic wrap (so that the dough doesn't dry out while you shape the bread sticks). Run 1 piece through the pasta machine on the thickest setting, which will flatten it enough. Then run the sheet through the machine on the fettuccine setting. Separate the strands of dough, then set them on the baking sheets just a little bit apart from each other (they won't rise or spread much).

As soon as the first sheet is filled up, bake for 15 minutes, while you roll and cut the remaining dough pieces.

5. Continue to bake and cut until you've used all of the dough, transferring the baked bread sticks to a wire rack to cool. Store the bread sticks in an airtight container at room temperature for up to 1 week. To prepare bread sticks for longer shelf life, see below.

VARIATION

EXTRA-CRISP BREAD STICKS

Like biscotti, bread sticks can be twice-baked for extra crispness. This is a good idea if you plan on keeping them for a while. Drying them out in the oven will prevent them from getting soggy over the course of a few days of storage. Simply place the cooled bread sticks on a baking sheet in a single layer and bake them at 250°F for 1 hour. Cool completely before storing in an airtight container for up to 3 weeks.

CIABATTA ROLLS

Not only are these rolls a fixture in my bread basket, but they are also my go-to sandwich rolls. Made with airy *ciabatta* dough, they are bubbly to the point of ethereal, but with a crust sturdy enough to be picked up with two hands. *Ciabatta* Rolls are a great showcase for all kinds of sandwich fillings and won't overpower even the lightest combinations. Lately, my favorite consists of a handful of fluffy arugula, a thin slice of prosciutto, some shredded carrot, a drizzle of lemon juice and olive oil, and a sprinkling of sea salt.

Ciabatta dough is so light and bubbly because it is very wet. It is impossible to knead by hand without adding too much flour (a relatively new Italian bread, it was invented for the mixer). I use *biga*, the traditional Italian pre-ferment (see "Baker's Favorite: *Biga*" on page 65), because it is always used in *ciabatta* in Italy, and it vastly improves the flavor and the texture of the rolls. Once it has risen, take care not to deflate its air cells. Gently cut it into rustic pieces and barely handle them at all before proofing and baking.

FOR THE *BIGA*

4.37 ounces/124 grams (½ cup) room temperature water (70°F to 78°F)

.03 ounce/.75 gram (¼ teaspoon) instant yeast

7.05 ounces/200 grams (1½ cups) unbleached bread flour

FOR THE DOUGH

8 ounces/240 grams (1 cup) water

.05 ounce/1.5 grams (½ teaspoon) instant yeast

10.59 ounces/300 grams (2¼ cups) unbleached all-purpose flour

.21 ounce/6 grams (1 teaspoon) fine sea salt or kosher salt

1. **Make the *biga*:** Pour the water into a mixing bowl. Add the yeast and flour and stir with a rubber spatula just until all the water is absorbed and a rough dough forms. Turn the *biga* into another oiled bowl, cover with plastic wrap, and let stand at room temperature for 1 hour, before refrigerating for at least 12 hours and up to 16 hours. The *biga* will double in volume, become porous, and smell tangy.

2. **Make the dough:** Pour the water into the bowl of a standing mixer. Add the yeast, flour, and salt. Stir with a rubber spatula until a rough dough forms. Using a standing mixer fitted with the dough, knead the dough on low speed, adding the *biga* in 4 portions. When all of the *biga* has been added, turn the mixer to medium speed and knead until it is creamy-looking, shiny, and elastic, 4 to 5 minutes.

3. Transfer the dough to a lightly oiled bowl or dough-rising container, cover the bowl with plastic wrap, and let stand at room temperature until it has tripled in volume, 3 to 3½ hours.

4. Give the dough 2 turns: Flour your hands, and then scoop up the dough from the sides. Let it droop down and then place the dough back into the bowl, allowing the drooping sides to flop toward the center. Gently pat the dough down, and then repeat.

5. Line a baker's peel or a rimless baking sheet with a piece of parchment paper. Turn the dough out onto a lightly floured countertop and pat into an 8-inch square. Cut the square into two 8 by 4-inch rectangles. Cut each rectangle into four 4 by 2-inch pieces. Transfer the pieces to the prepared peel or baking sheet, separating them by at least 2 inches. Sprinkle them lightly with flour and drape with plastic wrap. Let stand until puffy and increased in volume by 1½ times, about 1½ hours.

6. One hour before baking, place a baking stone on the middle rack of the oven. Preheat the oven to 450°F.

7. Slide the rolls, still on the parchment, onto the preheated baking stone. Bake until they are nicely browned, 18 to 20 minutes.

8. Slide the peel or the rimless baking sheet under the parchment paper to remove the rolls from the oven. Cool for about 5 minutes on a wire rack, and then peel them off the parchment paper. *Ciabatta* Rolls will keep at room temperature in an airtight container for up to 1 day. For longer storage, freeze in a zipper-lock plastic bag for up to 1 month. To defrost, place on the countertop for an hour or two, and reheat in the oven at 350°F for 5 minutes before serving.

CIABATTA WITH BRAN

Italian bakers occasionally sprinkle the tops and bottoms of their breads with wheat bran, instead of cornmeal or flour, to prevent sticking. I love the rugged look of the bran, but I also like the flavor and texture it gives to white breads. So sometimes I sprinkle the parchment-lined peel and the tops of the rolls with bran and stir .53 ounce/15 grams (2 tablespoons) of wheat bran into my *ciabatta* dough (along with the flour) as well.

SEVEN-SEED CIABATTA ROLLS

For healthful and flavorful *ciabatta* rolls, add a mixture of seeds and grains. Combine 1 teaspoon each of poppy seeds, sesame seeds, flax seeds, sunflower seeds, pine nuts, buckwheat groats, instant oats, and millet in a small bowl. Add half of the mixture to the dough along with the other ingredients. After shaping, lightly brush each roll with a little water and sprinkle the remaining seeds on the tops. Use whatever seeds and grains you have on hand to make up a scant 2 tablespoons.

BAKER'S FAVORITE: *BIGA*

Although I bake a considerable number of sourdough breads at Bread Alone, I also use *biga*, an Italian-style pre-ferment, just as often. What do breads get from *biga*? Some of the same benefits they'd get from a sourdough starter: great flavor, bubbly crumb, a shiny and caramelized crust, and an increased shelf life. One thing they don't get is the hint of acidity that you taste in even the mildest sourdough bread. I'm convinced that the peasant bread and *ciabatta* breads at my bakery are customer favorites because of their crowd-pleasing flavor.

This stiff dough starter made with commercial yeast, a tradition in Italian bakeries, is much quicker and easier to make than a sourdough starter. Just knead together some flour, water, and yeast. After a half a day (compare this to the 10 or more days you'd need to cultivate a sourdough starter), it's ready to raise bread. Because it is a very dry mixture that ferments slowly at a cool temperature, there's little chance of over-fermentation. So if you're not ready to bake when your *biga* is ready, leave it in the refrigerator for up to 12 hours longer and it will still raise your bread beautifully.

GRILLED SAVORY OR
SWEET *CIABATTA*

Grilled pizza is a family favorite. One day when I was mixing a big batch of *ciabatta* dough, I realized that it had the same feel as pizza dough, but without the oil. Why not throw some on the grill and see what would happen? The result was a deliciously bubbly grilled flatbread, too airy and soft to stand up to heavy fillings but perfect as a casual bread to serve alongside any other grilled foods. The sweet version (less filling than a Danish, not as serious as a bagel) is a great breakfast bread or picnic snack for hungry kids with a sweet tooth.

If you're making the salt-and-pepper version, take care to use freshly ground pepper and your favorite sea salt. On grilled *ciabatta*, I always use Maldon® salt from England. It's available at my rural grocery story, so you should look for it where you shop. Or order it online; it's worth it (see Resources on page 134). The large, flaky crystals add crunch as well as flavor.

FOR THE *BIGA*

4.37 ounces/124 grams (½ cup) room temperature water (70°F to 78°F)

.03 ounce/.75 gram (¼ teaspoon) instant yeast

6.75 ounces/200 grams (1½ cups) unbleached bread flour

FOR THE DOUGH

8 ounces/240 grams (1 cup) room temperature water (70°F to 78°F)

.05 ounce/1.5 grams (½ teaspoon) instant yeast

10.59 ounces/300 grams (2½ cups) unbleached all-purpose flour

.16 ounce/5 grams (1 teaspoon) fine sea salt or kosher salt

Best-quality sea salt and freshly ground black pepper

or

Granulated sugar

1. **Make the *biga*:** Pour the water into a medium bowl. Add the yeast and flour and give the mixture a few turns with a rubber spatula to moisten the flour. The *biga* will be stiff and dense. Turn the *biga* into an oiled bowl, and cover with plastic wrap. Let stand at room temperature for 1 hour, and then refrigerate for 12 to 16 hours. The *biga* will double in volume, become porous, and smell tangy.

2. **Make the dough:** Pour the water into the bowl of a standing mixer. Add the yeast, flour, and salt. Stir with a rubber spatula until a rough dough forms. Using a standing mixer fitted with the dough, knead the dough on low speed, adding the *biga* in 4 portions. When all of the *biga* has been added, turn the mixer to medium speed and knead until it is creamy-looking, shiny, and elastic, 4 to 5 minutes.

3. Transfer the dough to a lightly oiled bowl or dough-rising container, cover the bowl with plastic wrap, and let stand at room temperature for 1½ hours.

4. Give the dough 2 turns: Flour your hands, and then scoop up the dough from the sides. Let it droop down and then place the dough back into the bowl, allowing the drooping sides to flop toward the center. Gently pat the dough down, and then repeat. Cover and let stand until it has risen voluminously, at least doubling in volume, another 1½ to 2 hours.

5. Line 2 baking sheets with parchment paper and sprinkle them liberally with flour. Sprinkle a work surface liberally with flour. Invert the dough onto the work surface and gently pat it into an 8-inch square.

6. Use a bench scraper or sharp chef's knife to cut the dough into four 4-inch-wide pieces, and then cut each piece into 2-inch pieces. Place the pieces on the baking sheets, at least 1 inch apart. Brush them lightly with water and then sprinkle liberally with either salt and pepper or sugar. Drape the pieces with plastic wrap and let stand for 1½ hours.

7. Preheat a gas grill on medium for at least 10 minutes or prepare a charcoal fire with medium-hot glowing coals (alternatively, preheat a stovetop griddle over medium heat). Oil the grill grids. Gently transfer the rolls from the baking sheets to the hot grill and cook until toasty brown, about 5 minutes. Turn and cook until the other side is equally toasty, 4 to 5 minutes more. Serve hot from the grill, warm, or at room temperature. Grilled Savory or Sweet *Ciabatta* is best eaten on the day it is made.

NAVAJO FRY BREAD

There is a long tradition of Native American fried bread recipes. The most well-known is Navajo Fry Bread, which became famous as a staple on reservations. Supplied with flour, powdered milk, and lard, resourceful cooks produced this classic bread. My version includes a little yeast, which lightens up the dough and gives it a more complex flavor. I bet the breads would taste great fried in lard, but I fry mine in vegetable oil for health reasons. They are great enjoyed hot from the pot. Or let them cool slightly and stuff them with meat and vegetables, or tear them into pieces and dip into them hummus or another earthy bean dip.

17.64 ounces/500 grams (4 cups) unbleached all-purpose flour

.11 ounce/3 grams (¾ teaspoon) fine sea salt

.64 ounce/20 grams (1 tablespoon plus 1 teaspoon) instant yeast

2 ounces/61 grams (¼ cup) room temperature milk (70°F to 78°F)

15.34 ounces/435 grams (1¾ cups) room temperature water (70°F to 78°F)

Vegetable oil, for frying

1. Combine the flour, salt, and yeast in the bowl of a standing mixer fitted with the paddle attachment. Add the milk and water and beat on medium speed until well-combined, scraping down the sides of the bowl once or twice as necessary.

2. Transfer the dough to a lightly oiled bowl or dough-rising container, cover the bowl with plastic wrap, and let stand at room temperature until it doubles in volume, 2½ to 3 hours.

3. Line a baking sheet with parchment paper and dust the parchment with flour. Liberally dust a work surface with flour and turn the dough out onto it. Divide the dough into 10 equal pieces and shape each one into a round (see "Instructions for Shaping Rounds" on page 44). Place the dough balls on the prepared baking sheet, dust the tops with flour, and drape with plastic wrap. Let stand until slightly risen, 25 to 30 minutes.

4. Stretch each ball, as you would with pizza dough, into a flat 6-inch disk. Line another baking sheet with paper towels. Heat 1 inch of vegetable oil in a large, deep cast-iron skillet over medium-high heat to 350°F. Place the balls, 2 or 3 at a time, in the pan and fry until golden, turning once, about 8 minutes total.

Remove the fry bread from the pan with a slotted spoon and drain briefly on paper towels before serving warm.

VARIATION

CHILI-DUSTED NAVAJO FRY BREAD

You can easily add some Southwestern flavor to your breads with a spice mixture. Combine 2 teaspoons of chili powder, 1 teaspoon of sugar, 1 teaspoon of salt, 1 teaspoon of cumin, ½ teaspoon of coriander, and ½ teaspoon of cayenne in a small bowl. Sprinkle the mixture over your breads as they drain on the paper towels and while they are still very hot.

WHOLE WHEAT CHALLAH WITH APRICOTS

As an organic baker specializing in whole grain breads, I often wondered what challah would taste like if made with stone-ground whole wheat flour. This may sound outlandish, considering that challah is the whitest of white breads. But it makes sense if you remember that observant Jews baked and ate this bread hundreds of years ago, before millers began to sift the bran from flour, and all flour was whole wheat. So I went ahead and developed this recipe. Since I was already bucking the norm, I decided to add some chopped apricots to temper the bite of the whole wheat. The result is worthy of any occasion, including a Passover dinner.

Instead of braiding the dough, you may divide it and bake it in two greased 9 by 5-inch loaf pans or shape it into a round (see "Instructions for Shaping Rounds" on page 44) and bake it on a baking stone. Loaf pan challah is wonderful sliced and battered to make French toast.

8.47 ounces/240 grams (2 cups) whole wheat flour, preferably stone-ground

7.23 ounces/219 grams (1¾ cups) unbleached all-purpose flour

.23 ounce/7 grams (2¼ teaspoons) instant yeast

.24 ounce/7.5 grams (1½ teaspoons) fine sea salt or kosher salt

5.68 ounces/161 grams (¾ cup) room temperature water (70°F to 78°F)

3 large eggs, at room temperature

3.81 ounces/108 grams (½ cup) olive oil

1.76 ounces/50 grams (¼ cup) honey

1 ounce/30 grams (¼ cup) finely chopped dried apricots

1. Combine the whole wheat flour, all-purpose flour, yeast, sea salt, water, 2 of the eggs, olive oil, and honey in the bowl of a standing mixer fitted with a dough hook. Give the mixture a few turns with a rubber spatula to moisten all of the ingredients, and then knead on medium-high speed until your dough is smooth, 4 to 6 minutes. It will cling to the hook and clear the sides of the bowl. Add the apricots and knead until they're just incorporated, another minute or two.

2. Transfer the dough to a lightly oiled bowl or dough-rising container, cover the bowl with plastic wrap, and let stand at room temperature until it has doubled in volume, 1½ to 2 hours.

3. Gently press on the dough while it's still in the bowl to deflate it, and then turn it onto a lightly floured countertop. Divide it into 3 equal portions and, with the palms of your hands, roll each portion into a 15-inch-long rope, just the way you used to roll clay into ropes when you were a kid.

4. Line a baking sheet with parchment paper and place the 3 dough ropes side by side on the sheet. Pinch the ropes together at one end, tucking them under the loaf. Braid the ropes together, right over center and then left over center, as tightly as you can, until the ropes are too short to braid. Pinch the ends of the braid together and tuck them under the loaf as you did with the other end.

5. Dust the loaf lightly with flour, drape with plastic wrap, and let rise at room temperature until almost doubled in volume, 1 to 2 hours (alternatively, refrigerate the covered loaf overnight and bring it to room temperature before letting it rise completely).

6. Preheat the oven to 350°F. Lightly beat the remaining egg and brush it all over the top of the loaf. Bake the challah until the top is deep golden brown and the bottom makes a hollow sound when tapped, about 40 minutes. Transfer the bread to a wire rack to cool completely before slicing and serving. Whole Wheat Challah with Apricots will keep at room temperature in an airtight container for up to 2 days. For longer storage, freeze in a zipper-lock plastic bag for up to 1 month. To defrost, place on the countertop for an hour or two, and reheat in the oven at 350°F for 5 minutes before serving.

WHOLE WHEAT CHALLAH WITH GREEN OLIVES

Replace the apricots with .53 ounce/15 grams
(1 tablespoon) finely chopped pitted green
olives (any green olive will work here, but I
love big, juicy Cerignolas) for a savory version
of whole wheat challah, and serve with roast
chicken or brisket.

FLAVOR-PACKED FLATBREADS

I LOVE A LOT OF THINGS about flatbreads. First of all, there is their crust-to-crumb ratio. For people like me, who relish the chewy, caramelized exterior of a well-made bread, flatbreads are heaven. Second, many flatbreads contain a savory flavoring element: a sprinkling of chopped tomatoes and mozzarella cheese on a Neapolitan pizza, deeply browned onions on an Alsatian tart, or za'atar on my daughter's favorite Middle Eastern *Mana'eesh* (page 89).

Even plain flatbreads are often employed primarily as a container or base for a savory filling or topping: Think pita bread stuffed with falafel or naan with tandoori chicken. The savory element gives the flatbread enough substance and complexity to be considered a meal in itself. If you are a baker, you've got to love that!

These breads are as fun to make as they are to eat. Most flatbread recipes are flexible and improvisational. Rather than fitting your day around baking bread (as you would have to do when making, say, a traditional European artisan country bread), you can fit your baking into whatever you have planned for the day. After just a few minutes of kneading (flatbreads don't require long kneading to develop a strong gluten structure, since they don't have to rise high in the oven), many flatbread doughs can be fermented for as little as an hour or as long as a day before being shaped and baked whenever it's convenient. Setting the dough aside and paying no attention to it at all while you go about your daily routine is often a good idea. Letting flatbread dough rest for a nice long time allows the gluten to relax. Shaping becomes a snap. It is easy to stretch, pull, or roll such relaxed dough into a flattened round. Here is where flatbreads provide instant gratification: Most are baked as soon as they are shaped, so there's no waiting around for them to proof.

It was really hard to pick just a few recipes to feature here, but I managed to narrow the choices down to some of my absolute favorites, including a versatile pizza dough developed especially for the grill, a specialty flatbread influenced by my travels in the Alsace region of France, and a Middle Eastern flatbread recipe brought home from Israel by my daughter, who has a master's degree in Middle Eastern Studies from the University of Chicago and is a fine baker in her own right.

After a long day at my bakery, where I rigorously apply everything I know about baking science and am constantly striving to keep up with the industry's latest technological innovations, it is a pleasure to come home and throw some pizza dough on the grill, cooking it over an open flame the way people first cooked breads hundreds, if not thousands, of years ago.

With flatbreads, I can be spontaneous, satisfying my cravings or improvising with ingredients in a way that I can't with most of the classic bread recipes I use at work. I usually don't decide how to top my pizza until the grill is heating and I have a chance to check out what's in the fridge or ready from the garden.

Sometimes I'll make *Mana'eesh* the traditional way, topped with an egg and a sprinkling of dried sumac, but sometimes I'll substitute fresh rosemary for the sumac and throw some Parmesan shavings over the breads, giving them a decidedly Western Mediterranean flavor. These are my "baker's holiday" breads, since they require so little work and are so much fun to make and eat. Take a break from serious baking and grill some pizza tonight to see what I mean.

PIZZA DOUGH FOR GRILLING

Brick-oven traditionalist that I am, when I first started hearing about grilled pizza it seemed like a fad. But since I love to grill in the summertime, it wasn't long before I had to give it a try. One pizza later, I was hooked. Even the burliest barbecue king will feel the same way, draping the silky, wet dough over the grill and watching it instantly puff and solidify, its underside quickly becoming golden, with eye-catching grill marks.

Once this happens, it is simple to flip the dough. Then you have a flat surface upon which to brush some oil or even a light sauce and sprinkle some sea salt and some cracked black pepper before pulling it off the grill to serve as an appetizer while your chicken or steaks are cooking.

I use a portion of Italian-style *tipo 00* flour from King Arthur (see Resources on page 134) for an authentic Italian texture (some all-purpose flour is necessary or the dough will be too soft), but using all unbleached all-purpose flour works very well, too.

14.64 ounces/415 grams (3 cups) Italian-style *tipo 00* flour

3 ounces/85 grams (¾ cup) unbleached all-purpose flour

.6 ounce/18 grams (2 tablespoons) instant yeast

.16 ounce/5 grams (1 teaspoon) fine sea salt or kosher salt

12 ounces/345 grams (1½ cups) room temperature water (70°F to 78°F)

.71 ounce/20 grams (1 tablespoon) olive oil

1. At least 1 hour and up to 24 hours before you plan on grilling, make the dough: Combine the *tipo oo* flour, all-purpose flour, yeast, and salt in the bowl of a standing mixer fitted with a dough hook. Add the water and olive oil and give the mixture a few turns with a rubber spatula until a rough dough forms. Mix on medium speed until the dough is smooth and silky, 3 to 4 minutes.

2. Transfer the dough to a lightly oiled bowl or dough-rising container, cover the bowl with plastic wrap, and let stand at room temperature for up to 1½ hours. If you aren't going to use the dough immediately, refrigerate until you need it, for up to 1 day.

3. Build a wood or charcoal fire, allowing the coals to remain red hot and close to the grill rack. Or preheat a gas grill to high, with the lid down.

4. Prepare an outdoor work surface on a table near your grill. Place a large, generously oiled baking sheet on the table.

5. Bring the pizza dough to the table. Turn it onto the baking sheet and use oiled hands to coax it into a flat shape. The dough will be quite fragile, so don't make it too thin; it should be at least ⅛ inch thick. You want to be able to lift the dough and place it on the grill without it tearing. Grasp one end of the pizza with the fingertips of both hands and guide it swiftly as you allow the edge of the dough to fall on the hot grill. Pull on it slightly as you place the dough all the way onto the grill and release it. You will no doubt have created an artful shape.

6. Cook the pizza uncovered until it is golden, with blackened grid marks, on the bottom, 2 to 3 minutes, peeking underneath often to make sure it is not burning. Use tongs to flip the dough over and slide it to a cooler part of your grill. Apply any toppings of your choice, cover the grill, and cook until the toppings are heated through and the bottom is well-browned, a few minutes longer. Slide the pizza onto a peel or back onto the baking sheet, slice, and serve.

VARIATION

PIZZA DOUGH WITH HONEY AND WINE

If you replace some of the water in Pizza Dough for Grilling with white wine and add a little honey, you will create a versatile and deliciously flavored dough. Brush it with some fruity olive oil, some flaky Maldon sea salt, and a handful of fresh rosemary leaves, and enjoy with a glass of Riesling in the early fall to celebrate the harvest. Or top it with some fresh tomato sauce and homemade (or handmade from your favorite gourmet store) ricotta cheese. Or top with sautéed broccolini, provolone, and hot red peppers.

To make Pizza Dough with Honey and Wine, use 9.35 ounces/265 grams (1¼ cups) of water and 2.83 ounces/80 grams (⅓ cup) of dry white wine, and add 1 tablespoon of honey to the dough along with the water and the wine. Grill as directed and top as you like.

GRAPE *SCHIACCIATA*

This is one of those seasonal recipes that I can't wait to make each fall, when tiny champagne grapes (also known as Black Corinth grapes) are briefly available at my local farm stand. After a casual meal, I serve squares of this traditional Tuscan flatbread with a selection of Italian cheeses, including an aged pecorino and a soft taleggio (or some of the soft goat cheese I get from my friend Lisa's farm), and small glasses of sweet Vin Santo instead of dessert. If champagne grapes are not available, don't be tempted to use regular table grapes. They have a nice crunch when you eat them out of hand, but they have more water than flavor inside. Instead, try the variations on page 84, which also pay homage to Tuscany and also pair well with cheese and Italian dessert wine.

15.67 ounces/444 grams (3½ cups) unbleached all-purpose flour

.23 ounce/6.75 grams (2¼ teaspoons) instant yeast

.08 ounce/2.54 grams (½ teaspoon) fine sea salt or kosher salt

.78 ounce/22 grams (1 tablespoon) honey

1.25 ounce/36 grams (2½ tablespoons) olive oil

.78 ounce/22 grams (1 tablespoon) red wine

1 large egg

8 ounces/240 grams (1 cup) water

1 teaspoon grated orange zest

20 ounces/505 grams (3 cups) champagne or Concord grapes

1. Combine the flour, yeast, salt, honey, oil, wine, egg, water, and orange zest in the bowl of a standing mixer fitted with a dough hook. Give the mixture a few turns with a rubber spatula until a rough dough forms. Knead on medium-high speed until smooth and silky, 6 to 8 minutes.

2. Transfer the dough to a lightly oiled bowl or dough-rising container, cover the bowl with plastic wrap, and let stand at room temperature for up to 1½ hours.

3. Oil the bottom and sides of a rimmed baking sheet. Turn the dough onto a lightly floured countertop and divide into 2 equal pieces. With a floured rolling pin, roll 1 of the pieces into a rectangle measuring about 15 by 12 inches. Place the rectangle on the prepared baking sheet and press the dough so that it covers the bottom and comes up the sides of the sheet.

4. Sprinkle three-quarters of the grapes evenly over the dough. Roll out the remaining piece of dough and place it on top of the grapes, stretching it to cover. Sprinkle the remaining grapes evenly over the dough. Allow the *schiacciata* to sit, uncovered, for 20 minutes.

5. Preheat the oven to 400°F. Bake the *schiacciata* in the middle of the oven until well-browned, 45 to 50 minutes. Let cool on the baking sheet for 10 minutes, and then lift it with a large spatula onto a wire rack to cool completely before cutting into squares. Grape *Schiacciata* will keep at room temperature in an airtight container for up to 2 days.

VARIATIONS

ROSEMARY-WALNUT SCHIACCIATA

Replace the orange zest with 3.75 ounces/ 15 grams (2 tablespoons) of fresh rosemary and the grapes with 7 ounces/200 grams (1¾ cups) of walnuts, chopped.

CHERRY TOMATO–ANISE SCHIACCIATA

Replace the orange zest with 3.75 ounces/ 15 grams (2 tablespoons) of anise seeds and the grapes with 18 ounces/500 grams (3½ cups) of cherry tomatoes.

SO YOU WANT TO KNEAD BY HAND . . .

I developed most of the recipes in this book with the idea that using a standing mixer is the quickest and easiest way to knead bread dough. Certainly, you are better off kneading very wet doughs like those for *Ciabatta* Rolls (page 63) or Pizza Dough for Grilling (page 78) by machine. Kneading them by hand is messy, and it is easy to succumb to the temptation to add too much flour as you knead, the result being a dry, tight, under-risen bread. By the same token, very stiff doughs such as the ones for Authentic Bagels (page 45) or Boiceville Bialys (page 41) can be tough on your hands and forearms. The tendency is to under-knead these stiff doughs, just because it's such hard work.

But I recommend that every home baker try to hand-knead bread dough a couple of times. It's a great way to get to know your dough as it develops from a ragged lump into a smooth, elastic mass. If you'd like to actually feel the proteins in the flour organizing themselves into a gluten web beneath your hands, try hand-kneading *schiacciata* dough (see page 82), which is easy and fun to work with. Here are some tips on how to do it.

• **Give Yourself Some Space** Lightly flour a countertop space at least 2 feet square and low enough so that you can extend your arms and use your body weight to manipulate the dough.

• **Push, Fold, and Turn** Turn the dough out onto the countertop. Lightly flour your hands (alternatively, you could rub some olive oil onto them) rather than sprinkling the dough with flour. Knead the dough by pushing it down and forward with the heels of your hands, and then fold the dough back on itself and push again. After every fold, turn the dough clockwise on the counter, for even kneading, and repeat.

• **Take Frequent Breaks** It's okay to stop for a minute if you get tired. In fact, during that time, the gluten in your dough will be doing some of your work for you, organizing itself into a coherent web while you rest.

• **Know When You're Done** Different recipes will give you different kneading guidelines. Some doughs, like *schiacciata* (see page 82), should progress from raggedy to smooth and silky before you set them aside to ferment. Others, such as *Mana'eesh* (page 89), should only be briefly kneaded but left rather rough, so that they won't bubble up too much during baking. Evaluate your dough periodically as you knead, so that you can stop at the right time.

SAVORY YEASTED TART WITH ONION CONFIT AND OLIVES

This is an absolutely delicious flatbread that you can serve as either a light main course or an appetizer. Unlike leaner pizza and focaccia doughs, this dough is enriched with milk, butter, eggs, and olive oil, for exceptional tenderness and flavor. The slow-cooked onion topping is exquisitely caramelized. Oil-cured olives add a bracing saltiness to the rich tart.

Onions and olives are a classic pairing, but you could substitute thick-cut bacon bits or chopped anchovies for the olives, if you'd like. Or add some sliced yellow and red bell peppers to the pan midway through cooking the onions, for another colorful and tasty variation.

FOR THE DOUGH

11.29 ounces/320 grams (¾ cup) room temperature whole milk (70°F to 78°F)

1.5 ounces/42 grams (3 tablespoons) unsalted butter

1 ounce/29 grams (1 tablespoon) olive oil

20.17 ounces/572 grams (4 cups) unbleached all-purpose flour

.2 ounce/6 grams (2 teaspoons) instant yeast

.16 ounce/5 grams (1 teaspoon) fine sea salt or kosher salt

2 large eggs

FOR THE TOPPING

.5 ounce/14 grams (1 tablespoon) unsalted butter

3 medium yellow onions (about 1½ pounds/680 grams), finely chopped

2 ounces/57 grams (¼ cup) heavy cream

1 garlic clove, finely chopped

10 or so fresh thyme leaves

.03 ounce/.7 gram (¼ teaspoon) sugar

Fine sea salt and freshly ground black pepper, to taste

¼ cup oil-cured olives, pitted and halved

I. **Make the dough:** Place the milk and butter in a small saucepan and heat over low heat, stirring occasionally, until the butter is melted. Remove from the heat and add the olive oil. Let cool to lukewarm.

2. Combine the flour, yeast, and salt in the bowl of a standing mixer fitted with a dough hook. Add the milk mixture and the eggs and give the mixture a few turns with a rubber spatula until a rough dough forms. Knead on medium speed until the dough is smooth, about 5 minutes. Cover the bowl with plastic wrap and let stand until the dough is doubled in volume, about 1½ hours.

3. **Make the topping:** Heat the butter in a large skillet over low heat. Add the onions, cover, and let cook until the onions are golden and very soft, lifting the lid to stir frequently, about 1 hour. Add the cream, garlic, thyme, sugar, and salt and pepper to taste, and let cool to room temperature.

4. Grease a rimmed baking sheet with butter. Turn the dough onto a lightly floured countertop and knead briefly. Use a rolling pin to roll it out, and then transfer it to the baking sheet and press it to fit.

5. Spread the onion confit evenly over the dough. Arrange the olives artfully on top of the onions. Cover the tart with plastic wrap and let stand at room temperature for 1 hour.

6. Preheat the oven to 350°F. Uncover the tart and bake until the crust is golden brown, 20 to 25 minutes. Let cool for 10 minutes on the baking sheet, and then use a large metal spatula to transfer the tart to a wire rack to cool. Slice and serve. Savory Yeasted Tart with Onion Confit and Olives will keep in an airtight container at room temperature for up to 2 days.

MANA'EESH

Since her undergraduate days, my daughter Liv has been traveling back and forth to the Middle East to study Arabic and Hebrew and to write about Arab-Israeli conflict and resolution. She introduced me to *mana'eesh*, the daily bread of the Eastern Mediterranean. In many rural villages, women still spend the early hours of the morning crouching over their low courtyard ovens, baking the day's bread.

As Liv traveled through Syria, Lebanon, Jordan, Israel, and Palestine, she sampled some delicious variations of this olive oil–rich bread, most often topped with za'atar, a mixture of dried thyme, sesame seeds, and sumac. During several trips to the Palestinian territories, she took some time to learn how to make the local flatbread, and she shared the recipe with me. What a perfect souvenir.

The dough is a simple mixture of flour, yeast, salt, and water. When we tinkered with the recipe back in the Catskills, we realized that too much kneading made the breads puff up like pita pockets. Since we wanted to pile chicken and onions on top of them or use them as a base for other toppings, we decided to knead the dough minimally, so that it would stay relatively flat as it baked. We also liked the tangy flavor of the dough when it fermented in the refrigerator overnight, although if you are in a hurry you can let it rise at room temperature (this should take just an hour or two) and bake the breads right away.

Liv ate versions of *mana'eesh* in all sizes. We give directions here for two sizes. The small version makes an exotic addition to the bread basket. Larger breads, topped with chicken and caramelized onions (see variation on page 95), make a simple but unbelievably flavorful dinner.

10 ounces/286 grams (2 cups) unbleached all-purpose flour

.1 ounce/4 grams (1⅛ teaspoons) instant yeast

.16 ounce/5 grams (1 teaspoon) fine sea salt or kosher salt

7 ounces/199 grams (¾ cup plus 2 tablespoons) room temperature water (70°F to 78°F)

4 ounces/113 grams (¼ cup) extra-virgin olive oil, plus more for brushing the breads

1.2 ounces/30 grams (1½ tablespoons) za'atar

1. Combine the flour, yeast, and salt in the bowl of a standing mixer fitted with a dough hook. Add the water and oil and give the mixture a few turns with a rubber spatula until a rough dough forms. Knead on medium speed until the dough comes together but is still a little ragged, about 7 minutes. Transfer the dough to a lightly oiled bowl or dough-rising container, cover the bowl with plastic wrap, and refrigerate overnight. It will double in volume.

2. One hour before you want to bake, remove the dough from the refrigerator. Turn it onto a lightly floured countertop and use a bench scraper or sharp chef's knife to divide it into 2 equal pieces for large flatbreads or 6 equal pieces for small ones. Shape the dough pieces into loose rounds (see "Instructions for Shaping Rounds" on page 44), sprinkle with flour, and drape with plastic wrap. Let stand until puffy and almost doubled in volume, 1 hour.

3. While the dough rounds are proofing, place a baking stone on the middle rack of the oven. Preheat the oven to 400°F.

4. Line a baker's peel with parchment paper. Use your hands to stretch the larger

MAKING YOUR OWN ZA'ATAR

Za'atar isn't a single spice but rather is a mixture of herbs, spices, sesame seeds, and salt. You can easily make za'atar, customizing it to your taste. Here is the ingredient combination that I use. Feel free to add more or less of any of the ingredients, or add marjoram and/or oregano, to make a za'atar that is right for your taste.

ZA'ATAR

MAKES ABOUT 1/3 CUP

2 tablespoons roasted sesame seeds

1/4 cup dried sumac

2 tablespoons dried thyme

1 teaspoon fine sea salt or kosher salt

Combine the sesame seeds, sumac, thyme, and salt in a small airtight container. Store in a cool, dry place for up to 6 months.

dough pieces into 8-inch circles or press the smaller ones into 3-inch circles. Place the dough circles on the parchment-lined peel. Press your fingertips into the dough rounds to create little dimples. Brush the rounds liberally with olive oil and sprinkle with za'atar.

5. Slide the dough, still on the parchment, onto the hot baking stone and bake until lightly browned, about 10 minutes for large breads, 7 minutes for small ones (don't overbake or they'll be too hard). Slide the breads, still on the parchment, onto a wire rack to cool slightly. Serve warm, or cool completely and serve at room temperature. *Mana'eesh* are best eaten on the day they are baked. For longer storage, freeze in a zipper-lock plastic bag for up to 1 month. To defrost, place on the countertop for 15 to 30 minutes, and reheat in the oven at 350°F for 5 minutes before serving.

VARIATION

MANA'EESH WITH BAKED EGGS

SERVES 2 FOR BREAKFAST OR LUNCH

If you ferment the dough in the refrigerator overnight, you can make these wonderful egg-topped flatbreads for breakfast or brunch the next morning. Sumac gives them a bright, lemony flavor that contrasts nicely with the richness of the egg. If you don't have sumac on hand, you may sprinkle ½ teaspoon of finely grated lemon zest over the breads as they come out of the oven. For a different but just as delicious version, sprinkle roasted sesame seeds and chopped fresh coriander (cilantro) over the breads as they come out of the oven. Or substitute a favorite dried herb, such as thyme, before baking. And there's no law that says you have to use Middle Eastern spices and herbs. Sometimes I use finely chopped fresh rosemary instead of the sumac, and in that case I shave some Parmesan onto the hot breads as soon as they are baked to give them an Italian flavor.

10 ounces/286 grams (2 cups) unbleached all-purpose flour

.1 ounce/4 grams (1⅛ teaspoons) instant yeast

.16 ounce/5 grams (1 teaspoon) fine sea salt or kosher salt, plus more for sprinkling

7 ounces/199 grams (¾ cup plus 2 tablespoons) room temperature water (70°F to 78°F)

4 ounces/113 grams (¼ cup) extra-virgin olive oil, plus more for brushing the breads

2 large eggs

.16 ounce/4 grams (½ teaspoon) dried sumac

1. Combine the flour, yeast, and salt in the bowl of a standing mixer fitted with a dough hook. Add the water and oil and give the mixture a few turns with a rubber spatula until a rough dough forms. Knead on medium speed until the dough comes together but is still a little ragged, about 7 minutes.

2. Transfer the dough to a lightly oiled bowl or dough-rising container, cover the bowl with plastic wrap, and refrigerate overnight. It will double in volume.

3. One hour before you want to bake, remove the dough from the refrigerator. Turn it onto a lightly floured countertop and use a bench scraper or sharp chef's knife to divide it into 2 equal pieces. Shape the dough pieces into loose rounds (see "Instructions for Shaping Rounds" on page 44), sprinkle with flour, and drape with plastic wrap. Let stand for 1 hour.

4. While the dough rounds are proofing, place a baking stone on the middle rack of the oven. Preheat the oven to 450°F.

5. Line a baker's peel with parchment paper. Lower the oven temperature to 400°F. Use your hands to stretch the dough pieces into 8-inch circles. Place the dough circles on the parchment-lined peel. Use the palm of your hand to form a depression in the center of each dough piece, to hold the egg. Brush the dough pieces liberally with olive oil.

6. Slide the dough, still on the parchment, onto the hot baking stone and carefully crack an egg into the depression of each dough round. Brush the dough around the egg with olive oil and sprinkle the egg and dough with sumac and salt. Bake until the egg is just set, about 7 minutes. Slide the flatbreads, still on the parchment, onto a wire rack, and then slide each bread onto a plate. Serve immediately.

MIDDLE EASTERN ENTRÉE

I'll let Liv introduce this chicken dish, which she discovered during her travels and taught me how to make on her return to the United States:

"During my first trip to the Middle East, I fell in love with the flavors and food culture I found in my time living with Israelis and Palestinians. My first Arabic teachers were women, young and old, who welcomed me into their kitchens and taught me the basics of a kitchen vocabulary: *zeitoon* (olives), *thum* (garlic), *khubz* (bread).

During a particularly memorable visit to a small Palestinian village in the hills north of Jerusalem, I first tasted *mousakhan*. This dish of flatbread layered with caramelized onions and chicken is an entrée. In this variation, I roast the chicken (traditionally it is boiled), and I've removed the chicken from the bone for a finger-friendly flatbread."

The last time Liv was visiting, we enjoyed the chicken and flatbread with a simple salad of cucumbers, tomatoes, and olives, dressed with lemon juice and olive oil.

MOUSAKHAN (PALESTINIAN CHICKEN AND ONIONS)

SERVES 4

¼ cup dried sumac

¼ teaspoon ground allspice

½ cup extra-virgin olive oil

8 medium onions (the size of your fists), peeled, halved, and thinly sliced

Fine sea salt or kosher salt and ground black pepper to taste

½ of a chicken (breast, wing, leg, and thigh, separated)

¼ cup pine nuts, toasted

2 large *Mana'eesh* (page 89)

1. Preheat the oven to 400°F. Combine the sumac and allspice in a small bowl.

2. Heat the oil in a large skillet or Dutch oven over low heat. Add the onions and cook, stirring occasionally, until they start to color, about 15 minutes. Stir in 1 tablespoon of the sumac mixture and salt and pepper to taste and continue to cook until the onions are a deep golden brown, about 15 minutes more.

3. While the onions are cooking, pat the chicken pieces dry. Sprinkle with salt and pepper and the remaining sumac mixture. Place the chicken in a baking dish and roast until cooked through, about 35 minutes. Let cool slightly, remove the meat from the bones, slice, and stir into the onions, along with the toasted pine nuts.

4. Place the *mana'eesh* on a baking sheet and pile a generous amount of the chicken and onion mixture on top of them. Place the baking sheet in the oven and bake until heated through, 3 to 5 minutes. Serve immediately.

QUICK
YEASTED TREATS

When most people think of sweet treats, their minds probably wander to cookies, cakes, and pies. But when *I* think of sweet treats, I remember the cider doughnuts I bought for my kids at the local farm stand or my grandmother's babka. There is a whole wonderful world of quick, easy yeasted treats with interesting flavors and textures to satisfy bakers with a sweet tooth. Yeast adds not only lightness to cakes and pastries but also a flavor dimension that sets a doughnut apart from and far above a muffin.

If you have never tasted a homemade yeasted coffee cake, be forewarned: Once you enjoy the incredible aroma and ethereal texture of Yeasted Coffee Cake with Fancy Pecan Topping (page 122), you may never make a coffee cake with baking powder again.

The recipes in this chapter represent a departure from my everyday baking life. At Bread Alone, I largely produce a variety of lean, rustic breads made with not much more than flour, water, yeast, and salt. Whole grain boules and sourdough baguettes are beautiful in their austerity, but sometimes a baker has to let loose. With the following recipes, I get to express a more excessive side of my baking personality. After a long week at the bakery, where I eat plenty of healthful sandwiches and whole grain breads paired with vegetable and bean soups, I love to spend the weekend in my kitchen at home, indulging in a breakfast of Yeasted Pancakes (page 99), treating my family to a batch of European-style jelly doughnuts called Berliners (page 103), or gathering friends around my table for coffee and a pull-apart Caramel Monkey Bread (page 127) that is so beautiful and delicious that it really should have a better name.

All of the breads that I bake and sell are certified organic, and anyone who knows me knows I have a passion for healthy eating. I would never buy a dozen doughnuts at a commercial bakery or grab a boxed coffee cake from a supermarket shelf. Health experts attribute the obesity epidemic to our reliance on easily accessible processed foods. People who cook and bake their own food simply don't get fat. My recipes for pancakes, waffles, and doughnuts are generally less fatty and sugary than recipes you'll find in other books, because I think that too much fat and sugar masks the wonderful flavor of yeasted dough.

Of course they are not low-fat or sugar-free, but I don't worry too much about the impact of a doughnut on my health. Following the advice of nutritionists and using common sense, I allow myself a doughnut when the urge strikes, *as long as I make it myself*. The healthiest way to enjoy Chocolate Babka (page 123) is the same way my grandmother enjoyed hers: taking the time on the occasional Sunday morning to make one by hand, and then sharing it with lucky family and friends.

YEASTED PANCAKES

I'll admit it. I am a pancake snob. Pancakes raised with baking powder or baking soda are just too heavy and doughy to meet my standards. Yeasted pancakes, in contrast, have a bubbly texture and a clean, slightly earthy (from the cinnamon) flavor that I can't resist. It is easy to make this batter just before bedtime, so that it is ready for the griddle when you are the next morning. Slow, cool fermentation gives the pancakes a tangy flavor that contrasts wonderfully with pure maple syrup. But there are many other ways to serve them. I love these pancakes as a base for two sunny-side-up eggs and some locally smoked bacon. Or I'll make fruit pancakes by sprinkling a few thin slices of banana and/or some fresh blueberries on each one as soon as it sets on the griddle. Or I'll sprinkle on some granola or muesli. These meals give me energy without weighing me down. The only thing left to do is put on my hiking boots or snowshoes and head outside.

In large quantities (more than ½ teaspoon per cup of flour), cinnamon may inhibit fermentation. But I can't imagine putting 2½ teaspoons (the amount that would potentially cause problems) into my pancake batter; ¾ teaspoon is plenty.

11.55 ounces/328 grams (2⅓ cups) unbleached all-purpose flour

.09 ounce/72 grams (¾ teaspoon) ground cinnamon

.25 ounce/7.5 grams (2½ teaspoons) instant yeast

.16 ounce/5 grams (1 teaspoon) fine sea salt or kosher salt

15 ounces/425 grams (1¾ cups) room temperature buttermilk (70°F to 78°F)

2.7 ounces/77 grams (¼ cup) honey

2.5 ounces/67 grams (5 tablespoons) unsalted butter, melted and cooled

2 large eggs, lightly beaten

.25 ounce/7 grams (1½ teaspoons) pure vanilla extract

1. Combine the flour, cinnamon, yeast, salt, buttermilk, honey, and butter in the bowl of a standing mixer fitted with the paddle attachment. Mix on low speed for a minute to moisten the ingredients, and then turn the mixer to medium speed and mix until the batter is smooth, 2 to 3 minutes. Cover the bowl with plastic wrap and refrigerate overnight.

2. Place a platter in the oven and preheat the oven to 200°F. Heat a griddle over medium-high heat. Stir the eggs and vanilla into the batter. Lightly grease the hot griddle with vegetable oil. Portion out the batter on the hot griddle (I like to use about ¼ cup per pancake), leaving an inch or two between the pancakes. Cook them until they're golden on their undersides and bubbly on top, and then flip and cook until their other sides are golden.

3. Transfer the pancakes to the heated platter and continue to cook until you've used all the batter, and then serve immediately (or just dish them out, hot from the griddle).

YEAST-RAISED WAFFLES

Here's an easy way to get your yeast-raised waffles batter smooth: Mix the dry and wet ingredients together in two stages. Leftover waffles freeze beautifully, double-wrapped in plastic wrap, for up to a month. Reheat them straight from the freezer in a toaster oven set at 350°F for 10 to 15 minutes. When searching for a waffle iron, it is well worth your while to choose a cast iron version because it is less "gadgety" than an electric one. My cast iron waffle iron took a little bit of getting used to, however, the result is an impeccable combination of crispy, crunchy, and moist crumb.

Also, to give these some whole grain flavor while keeping them nice and fluffy, stir 1 tablespoon of wheat germ into the flour mixture before making the batter. (See the variation that follows for a full-out whole grain version.)

3 large eggs, separated

17.63 ounces/500 grams (4 cups) unbleached all-purpose flour

3.53 ounces/100 grams (½ cup) sugar

.24 ounce/7.5 grams (1½ teaspoons) fine sea salt or kosher salt

25.8 ounces/732 grams (3 cups) room temperature whole milk (70°F to 78°F)

6 ounces/170 grams (1½ sticks) unsalted butter, melted and cooled

.28 ounce/8 grams (2 teaspoons) pure vanilla extract

.23 ounce/6.75 grams (2¼ teaspoons) instant yeast

1. Whip the egg whites together in the bowl of a standing mixer until soft peaks form. Set aside.

2. Whisk together the flour, sugar, and salt in a large mixing bowl. Whisk together the milk, egg yolks, melted butter, vanilla, and yeast in a medium bowl.

3. Combine half of the dry ingredients with half of the wet ingredients in another large bowl and mix thoroughly. Add the remaining dry and wet ingredients to the bowl and mix again until well-combined. Gently fold the egg whites into the batter, taking care not to deflate them.

4. Cover the bowl with plastic wrap and let stand until the batter has doubled in volume and become bubbly, about 1 hour. Stir with a rubber spatula to deflate.

5. Preheat the oven to 200°F. Preheat a waffle iron according to the manufacturer's instructions.

6. Pour some batter (how much depends on the size of your waffle iron) onto the grids and spread it to the edges with a spatula. Cook the waffles until they are golden brown, 4 to 7 minutes depending on your machine.

7. Keep the waffles warm in the oven on a platter loosely covered with aluminum foil until you use all the batter (or serve immediately, right from the waffle iron). Freeze leftover Yeast-Raised Waffles in a zipper-lock plastic bag for up to 1 month. To defrost, place on the countertop for 15 to 30 minutes, and reheat in a toaster or in the oven at 350°F for 10 to 15 minutes before serving.

VARIATION

WHOLE WHEAT AND FLAX SEED YEASTED WAFFLES

Flax seeds give these waffles a pleasant, slightly crunchy texture as well as a powerful nutritional boost. To make them, soak 3.33 ounces/37 grams (¼ cup) of flax seeds in 3.53 ounces/100 grams (¼ cup) of water for 30 minutes. Replace 2.2 ounces/62 grams (½ cup) of the white flour with stone-ground whole wheat flour. Stir the rehydrated flax seeds into the wet ingredients before mixing the batter.

JELLY-FILLED BERLINERS

Almost every bakery in Germany sells Berliners, which are similar to American jelly doughnuts but with a leaner, less sugary dough. To my palate, Berliners have a cleaner taste because of this formula. When I make these, I use either homemade preserves (see page 106 for recipes) or best-quality local jam that I buy at the local farm stand. If your jam is very chunky, purée it in a blender or small food processor so that it will pass without effort through the tip of a pastry bag and into the doughnut.

17.62 ounces/500 grams (4 cups) unbleached all-purpose flour

2.64 ounces/75 grams (⅓ cup) sugar, plus more for coating the Berliners

.65 ounce/13 grams (1 tablespoon plus 1½ teaspoons) instant yeast

.11 ounce/3 grams (¾ teaspoon) fine sea salt or kosher salt

8 ounces/245 grams (1 cup) room temperature milk (70°F to 78°F)

2.5 ounces/67 grams (5 tablespoons) unsalted butter, softened

2 large eggs

2 large egg yolks

.35 ounce/10 grams (1 teaspoon) grated lemon zest

.35 ounce/10 grams (2 teaspoons) pure vanilla extract

Vegetable oil, for frying

4.25 ounces/120 grams (6 tablespoons) raspberry jam

1. Combine the flour, sugar, yeast, salt, milk, butter, eggs, egg yolks, lemon zest, and vanilla in the bowl of a standing mixer fitted with the paddle attachment (the hook is not needed here, since this is a rather loose batter) and mix on low speed until smooth, 8 to 10 minutes.

2. Transfer the dough to a lightly oiled bowl or dough-rising container, cover the bowl with plastic wrap, and let stand at room temperature until doubled in volume, about 1 hour.

3. Line a rimmed baking sheet with parchment or waxed paper. Brush a thin layer of vegetable oil on the paper. Turn the dough onto a lightly floured countertop and divide into 16 equal pieces. Shape each piece into a round (see "Instructions for Shaping Rounds" on page 44) and then flatten slightly with the palm of your hand. Place the rounds seam side down on the oiled paper. Let stand uncovered at room temperature until doubled in volume, about 1 hour.

4. Add 3 inches of oil to a deep pot. Attach a candy thermometer to the side of the pot and heat the oil over medium heat until it reaches 350°F. Line a large platter or baking sheet with several layers of paper towels.

5. Place a few of the Berliners in the hot oil, being careful not to crowd them in the pot.

6. Fry until golden brown on one side, about 1 minute. Turn and continue to fry until golden on both sides, another minute or two. Don't worry that there is a line of light-colored dough around the perimeter of each Berliner. This will be the "soft spot" where you will insert the tip of a pastry bag to pipe in some jam. Drain the cooked Berliners on the paper towels, roll them in sugar, and repeat with the remaining dough, keeping an eye on the thermometer to make sure the oil stays at a steady 350°F and adjusting the heat as necessary.

7. To fill the Berliners, place the jam in a bowl and stir it thoroughly so that there are no lumps. Scrape it into a pastry bag fitted with a large plain tip. Insert the tip into the soft spot of each Berliner and squeeze about 1 teaspoon of the jam into the center. Serve immediately.

THREE EASY JAM RECIPES

I'd rather make jam in small batches to keep in the refrigerator for a couple of weeks than undertake the bigger and more complicated project of preserving large quantities of fruit for longer periods. These refrigerator jams will keep for up to 3 months, refrigerated in an airtight container. But they rarely last for more than 10 days in my house. I like to enjoy my jam when the fruit is in season and abundant: Strawberry Jam in June, Fig Jam and Peach and Rosemary Jam later in the summer.

The following recipes don't require added pectin, since I think it dilutes the flavor of the fruit. Strawberries, figs, and peaches have enough naturally occurring pectin to help the fruit set up on its own.

STRAWBERRY JAM

MAKES FOUR 8-OUNCE JARS

1 quart strawberries, hulled

½ cup sugar

¼ cup freshly squeezed lemon juice (from about 1 lemon)

1. Place the strawberries in the bowl of a food processor and pulse several times to coarsely chop.

2. Place the berries, sugar, and lemon juice in a heavy saucepan and cook over medium heat, stirring frequently, until the surface is covered with bubbles and the jam is thickened, about 10 minutes (to test the jam, place ¼ teaspoon of it on a cold plate; remove it from the heat when it is as spreadable as you like it).

3. Transfer the jam to clean glass jars and let cool to room temperature. Cover and refrigerate for up to 3 months.

FIG JAM

MAKES FOUR 8-OUNCE JARS

1 pound Mission or Calimyrna figs, stemmed and coarsely chopped

½ cup cider vinegar

1¾ cups sugar

1 tablespoon finely chopped fresh ginger (optional)

1. Combine the figs and vinegar in a heavy saucepan. Cook over very low heat until the juices from the fruit begin to flow, about 5 minutes. Turn the heat to medium to bring the jam to a simmer.

2. While the fruit is simmering, slowly stir in the sugar and then the ginger, if desired. Cook until set, about 30 minutes (to test the jam, place ¼ teaspoon of it on a cold plate; remove it from the heat when it is as spreadable as you like it).

3. Transfer the jam to clean glass jars and let cool to room temperature. Cover and refrigerate for up to 3 months.

PEACH AND ROSEMARY JAM

MAKES FOUR 8-OUNCE JARS

¼ cup freshly squeezed lemon juice (from about 1 lemon)

5 large peaches, peeled, pitted, and chopped

2½ cups sugar

1 sprig fresh rosemary

1. Sprinkle 2 tablespoons of the lemon juice over the peaches and set aside.

2. Combine the sugar and remaining 2 tablespoons of lemon juice in a heavy saucepan. Turn the heat to medium and bring to a boil, stirring often to keep the sugar from burning.

3. Carefully add the peaches and rosemary sprig to the hot sugar. Adjust the heat to bring the mixture to a lively simmer and cook until set, about 30 minutes (to test the jam, place ¼ teaspoon of it on a cold plate; remove it from the heat when it is as spreadable as you like it). Remove the rosemary sprig.

4. Transfer the jam to clean glass jars and let cool to room temperature. Cover and refrigerate for up to 3 months.

CIDER DOUGHNUTS

When my children were small, cider doughnuts were one of the only sweet treats they were allowed. How could I say no to such special yeasted pastries, especially when they were available only briefly in the fall? Now that the children are grown up and connoisseurs of all things sweet, including éclairs, tiramisu, and gelato, they still come running when I make these childhood favorites at home. The recipe is straightforward and relatively simple. Reducing the apple cider before adding it to the dough gives the doughnuts full apple flavor.

9.69 ounces/275 grams (1¼ cups) apple cider

17.62 ounces/500 grams (3½ cups) unbleached all-purpose flour

.1 ounce/3 grams (1 teaspoon) instant yeast

.09 ounce/2 grams (2 teaspoons) ground cinnamon

.13 ounce/4 grams (1⅓ teaspoons) fine sea salt or kosher salt

2.5 ounces/65 grams (5 tablespoons) unsalted butter, softened

8.11 ounces/230 grams (1 cup) sugar

3 large egg yolks

4.93 ounces/140 grams (⅔ cup) room temperature buttermilk (70°F to 78°F)

Vegetable oil, for frying

Cinnamon sugar (about ¼ cup should do it)

1. Bring the apple cider to a boil in a medium saucepan. Boil until it is reduced to ¼ cup, 7 to 10 minutes. Pour into a glass measuring cup and let cool to room temperature. Combine the flour, yeast, cinnamon, and salt in a medium bowl and set aside.

2. Place the butter and sugar in the bowl of a standing mixer fitted with the paddle attachment. Cream together on medium-high speed until well-combined, about 3 minutes, scraping down the sides of the bowl once or twice as necessary. Add the egg yolks and beat, scraping down the sides of the bowl once or twice as necessary, until smooth. Add the cooled cider and the buttermilk and beat until combined. Stir in the flour mixture until just combined. Do not overmix!

3. Transfer the dough to a lightly oiled bowl or dough-rising container, cover the bowl with plastic wrap, and let stand at room temperature until it is puffy and slightly risen, about 1½ hours.

4. Line 2 baking sheets with parchment or waxed paper and sprinkle generously with flour. Turn the dough out onto one of them and sprinkle the top of the dough with flour.

Flatten the dough with your hands until it is about ½ inch thick, sprinkling on more flour if necessary to prevent sticking. Place the baking sheet in the freezer until the dough is slightly hardened, about 20 minutes.

5. Remove the dough from the freezer and use a 3-inch doughnut cutter to cut as many doughnut shapes as you can. Place the cut doughnuts and the doughnut holes on the second baking sheet. Re-roll and cut the scraps. Refrigerate the cut doughnuts and holes for 20 to 30 minutes.

6. Add 3 inches of oil to a deep pot. Attach a candy thermometer to the side of the pot and heat the oil over medium heat until it reaches 350°F. Line a large platter or another baking sheet with several layers of paper towels.

7. Carefully add a few doughnuts to the pot, being careful not to crowd them. Fry until golden brown on one side, 30 seconds to 1 minute. Turn and continue to fry until golden on both sides, another 30 seconds to 1 minute. Drain the cooked doughnuts on the paper towels, and repeat with the remaining doughnuts, keeping an eye on the thermometer to make sure the oil stays

at a steady 350°F and adjusting the heat as necessary.

8. Roll the warm doughnuts in cinnamon sugar and serve warm.

VARIATION

GLAZED CIDER DOUGHNUTS

Whisk together 4 ounces/113 grams (½ cup) of apple cider with 8.47 ounces/240 grams (2 cups) of confectioners' sugar until smooth. Place the cooled doughnuts on a wire rack set over a rimmed baking sheet and pour the glaze over the doughnuts to coat the tops. Let them stand until the glaze has hardened, about 30 minutes, before serving.

BANANA DOUGHNUTS WITH MAPLE-WALNUT GLAZE

Doughnuts have become such a commercial commodity that tasting a freshly fried homemade example is a shock. At least, that was the case when I tested batches of these banana doughnuts at Bread Alone. The people who work here are quite jaded when it comes to eating handmade baked goods. But when the staff tried these, they went crazy. Roasting the bananas before mixing them into the dough concentrates their flavor and sweetness, giving them the appeal of the richest caramel.

Doughnuts made with roasted bananas have the most tantalizing taste and aroma. To give them some local flavor, we use pure New York State maple syrup made by a neighbor in the simple glaze. We keep saying that we are going to start selling them in small batches, fresh from the fryer, on Saturday mornings at one of our cafés, but they are really best made and enjoyed at home, where you can make them in *really* small batches for your favorite people.

Making the best yeast doughnuts requires a light touch. Knead the dough sufficiently, but don't over-knead it or you will develop too much gluten and wind up with a doughnut that's chewy rather than soft. Don't rush the dough during rising. Let it ferment long enough so that your doughnuts will puff up incredibly in the hot oil. Clean, hot canola oil (or any other flavorless vegetable oil) will give you a perfectly crisp exterior.

FOR THE DOUGH

11.29 ounces/320 grams (about 3 medium) ripe bananas, peeled and cut into bite-size pieces

3 ounces/84 grams (6 tablespoons) unsalted butter

1.13 ounces/32 grams (2 tablespoons) packed light brown sugar

14.11 ounces/400 grams (3¼ cups) unbleached all-purpose flour

.1 ounce/3 grams (1 teaspoon) instant yeast

.07 ounce/2 grams (½ teaspoon) ground cinnamon

.08 ounce/2.5 grams (½ teaspoon) fine sea salt or kosher salt

3.53 ounces/100 grams (½ cup) granulated sugar

2.12 ounces/60 grams (4 large) egg yolks

6 ounces/180 grams (¾ cup) room temperature buttermilk (70°F to 78°F)

Vegetable oil, for frying

FOR THE GLAZE

2.86 ounces/81 grams (⅓ cup) milk

3.53 ounces/100 grams (¼ cup) pure maple syrup

8.47 ounces/240 grams (2 cups) confectioners' sugar

3.52 ounces/100 grams (1 cup) toasted and chopped walnuts

1. **Make the dough:** Preheat the oven to 400°F. Combine the bananas, 1 ounce/28 grams (2 tablespoons) of the butter, and the brown sugar in an 8-inch-square baking dish. Bake until the bananas are browned and bubbly, about 8 minutes. Mash with a fork, leaving some chunks. Set aside to cool.

2. Combine the flour, yeast, cinnamon, and salt in a medium bowl.

3. Place the remaining 2 ounces/56 grams (4 tablespoons) of butter and the granulated sugar in the bowl of a standing mixer fitted with the paddle attachment. Cream together on medium-high speed until well-combined, about 3 minutes, scraping down the sides of the bowl once or twice as necessary. Add the egg yolks and beat, scraping down the sides of the bowl once or twice as necessary, until smooth. Add the cooled banana mixture and the buttermilk and beat until combined. Stir in the flour mixture until just combined. Do not overmix!

4. Transfer the dough to a lightly oiled bowl or dough-rising container, cover the bowl with plastic wrap, and let stand at room temperature until it is puffy and slightly risen, about 1½ hours.

5. Line 2 baking sheets with parchment or waxed paper and sprinkle generously with flour. Turn the dough out onto one of them and sprinkle the top of the dough with flour. Flatten the dough with your hands until it is about ½ inch thick, sprinkling on more flour if necessary to prevent sticking. Place the baking sheet in the freezer until the dough is slightly hardened, about 20 minutes.

6. Remove the dough from the freezer and use a 3-inch doughnut cutter to cut as many doughnut shapes as you can. Place the cut doughnuts and the doughnut holes on the second baking sheet. Re-roll and cut the scraps. Refrigerate the cut doughnuts and holes for 20 to 30 minutes.

7. Add 3 inches of oil to a deep pot. Attach a candy thermometer to the side of the pot and heat the oil over medium heat until it reaches 350°F. Line a large platter or another baking sheet with several layers of paper towels.

8. Carefully add a few doughnuts to the pot, being careful not to crowd them. Fry until golden brown on one side, 30 seconds to 1 minute. Turn and continue to fry until golden on both sides, another 30 seconds

to 1 minute. Drain the cooked doughnuts on the paper towels, and repeat with the remaining doughnuts, keeping an eye on the thermometer to make sure the oil stays at a steady 350°F and adjusting the heat as necessary.

9. **Make the glaze:** Whisk together the milk, maple syrup, and confectioners' sugar in a medium bowl until smooth. Place the cooled doughnuts on a wire rack set over a rimmed baking sheet and pour the glaze over the doughnuts to coat the tops. Sprinkle with the chopped nuts. Let them stand until the glaze has hardened, about 30 minutes, before serving.

STONE FRUIT BEIGNETS

These fruit fritters are more like desserts I've eaten in Germany and France over the years than traditional New Orleans beignets: small wedges of peach, apricot, plum, or nectarine, dipped in batter and briefly fried so that the fruit inside becomes warm, with caramelized edges, but still maintains its delightful freshness. Yeast in the batter makes the dough light and fragrant.

These beignets make a wonderful breakfast item or snack, but they can also be served for dessert with some fruit purée, crème fraîche, whipped cream, or ice cream. One thing they do have in common with their Cajun cousins: a heavy dusting of confectioners' sugar that makes them a little messy and a lot of fun to eat. For best results, use local fruit that's sweet and ripe (but not too soft or mushy). Feel free, in the fall, to use small apple or pear wedges in place of the stone fruits. In the summer, large stemmed strawberries would be great.

6.51 ounces/185 grams (1½ cups) unbleached all-purpose flour

1.63 ounces/46 grams (1 tablespoon) granulated sugar

.23 ounce/6.75 grams (2¼ teaspoons) instant yeast

.08 ounce/2.5 grams (½ teaspoon) fine sea salt or kosher salt

.26 ounce/7 grams (1½ teaspoons) pure vanilla extract

1 large egg

4 ounces/111 grams (½ cup) room temperature milk (70°F to 78°F)

2 ounces/61 grams (¼ cup) room temperature water (70°F to 78°F)

.65 ounce/18 grams (1 tablespoon plus 1 teaspoon) olive oil

Vegetable oil, for frying

8 to 10 peaches, nectarines, prune plums, or apricots, halved, pitted, and cut into 6 to 8 wedges each

Confectioners' sugar, for dusting

1. Combine the flour, granulated sugar, yeast, salt, vanilla, egg, milk, water, and olive oil in the bowl of a standing mixer fitted with the paddle attachment and mix on low speed until combined.

2. Transfer the batter to a lightly oiled bowl or dough-rising container, cover the bowl with plastic wrap, and let stand at room temperature for 1 hour (alternatively, cover the bowl and refrigerate for 8 to 20 hours).

3. Add 3 inches of oil to a deep pot. Attach a candy thermometer to the side of the pot and heat the oil over medium heat until it reaches 350°F. Line a large platter or baking sheet with several layers of paper towels.

4. Pat the fruit wedges dry with paper towels. Place 5 to 8 wedges in the bowl with the batter and turn to coat.

5. Carefully lift a fruit wedge out, allowing excess batter to drip back into the bowl. Place it in the hot oil. Repeat with the other wedges, in batches as necessary, being careful not to crowd them in the pot.

6. Fry until golden brown on one side, 30 seconds to 1 minute. Turn and continue to fry until golden on both sides, another 30 seconds to 1 minute. Drain the cooked beignets on the paper towels. Continue until all the fruit wedges are fried, keeping an eye on the thermometer to make sure the oil stays at a steady 350°F and adjusting the heat as necessary.

7. Dust the warm beignets generously with the confectioners' sugar and serve warm.

FONTINA *BOMBOLINI*

These small savory doughnuts are irresistible appetizers when served on their own or with homemade marinara sauce. They are also great as part of a vegetarian dinner, served alongside tomato soup or with selection of grilled vegetables that might include eggplant, zucchini, mushrooms, and peppers. I love Italian Fontina cheese, which has a silky texture and wonderfully nutty flavor when melted, but you could substitute another favorite firm cheese if you'd like. Unlike other doughnuts, which taste best right out of the fryer, these are almost as good the next day, either at room temperature or reheated in the oven at 350°F for 15 minutes.

19.02 ounces/539 grams (4¼ cups) unbleached bread flour

.76 ounce/22 grams (2 tablespoons) sugar

.3 ounce/9 grams (1 tablespoon) instant yeast

.16 ounce/5 grams (1 teaspoon) fine sea salt or kosher salt

8 ounces/245 grams (1 cup) room temperature milk (70°F to 78°F)

2.85 ounces/81 grams (6 tablespoons) unsalted butter, softened and cut into 6 pieces

3 large eggs

2 large egg yolks

2.85 ounces/81 grams Italian Fontina cheese, cut into ½-inch cubes (1 cup)

Vegetable oil, for frying

1. Combine the flour, sugar, yeast, salt, milk, butter, eggs, and egg yolks in the bowl of a standing mixer fitted with the paddle attachment and mix on low speed until smooth, 8 to 10 minutes. The dough will be sticky and quite tight.

2. Transfer the dough to a lightly oiled bowl or dough-rising container, cover the bowl with plastic wrap, and let stand at room temperature until just doubled in size, about 30 minutes. Give the dough 2 turns: With floured hands, scoop up the dough from underneath and let it droop over your hands. Place the dough back in the bowl with the drooping sides falling to the center of the bowl. Gently pat the dough down and then repeat this folding motion. Re-cover and let stand until it has doubled again, another 30 minutes.

3. Line a rimmed baking sheet with parchment or waxed paper. Brush a thin layer of vegetable oil on the paper. Turn the dough onto a lightly floured countertop and divide into 36 equal pieces. Shape each piece into a round (see "Instructions for Shaping Rounds" on page 44). With a sharp knife, pierce each round in the bottom center to create a pocket for a cheese cube. Settle the cube into the pocket and pinch the dough around the cheese together to seal. Place the rounds seam side down on the oiled paper. Let stand uncovered at room temperature until doubled in size, about 1 hour.

4. Add 4 to 5 inches of oil to a deep pot. Attach a candy thermometer to the side of the pot and heat the oil over medium heat until it reaches 350°F. Line a large platter or baking sheet with several layers of paper towels.

5. Place a few of the *bombolini* in the hot oil, being careful not to crowd them in the pot.

6. Fry until golden brown on one side, about 1 minute. Turn and continue to fry until golden on both sides, another minute or two. Remove the cooked *bombolini* from the oil with a slotted spoon and place on the lined baking sheet to drain. Repeat with the remaining dough, keeping an eye on the thermometer to make sure the oil stays at a steady 350°F and adjusting the heat as necessary. Serve hot. Fontina *Bombolini* will keep at room temperature in an airtight container for up to 1 day. Reheat in the oven at 350°F for 10 minutes before serving.

MARINARA DIPPING SAUCE

This beautifully simple sauce is a great dip for Fontina *Bombolini* (page 117), and it can also be used to top Pizza Dough for Grilling (page 78). Canning your homegrown San Marzano tomatoes is the best way to assure that you will always have the best sauce, however it is not always practical. There are several brands of canned, peeled whole tomatoes. Look for ones that specify the San Marzano tomato variety—they produce the meatiest sauces!

SIMPLE MARINARA SAUCE

MAKES ABOUT 3½ CUPS

¼ cup olive oil

4 cloves garlic, chopped

One 28-ounce can peeled chopped tomatoes, with juice

Salt and freshly ground black pepper, to taste

3 basil leaves, chopped, or 1 tablespoon prepared basil pesto

1. Heat the olive oil and garlic in a large saucepan over medium heat until the garlic is fragrant. Add the tomatoes and their juice. Season with salt and pepper to taste.

2. Bring the mixture to a boil. Lower the heat, and simmer until the sauce is thickened, about 20 minutes. Remove from the heat, stir in the basil or pesto, and adjust the seasonings as desired.

YEASTED COFFEE CAKE WITH SIMPLE ALMOND TOPPING

This is a marvelously simple yeasted coffee cake that is great for a crowd. Once you try it, you will want to make it over and over again, experimenting with toppings the way I do, using different kinds of nuts, sweeteners, and flavorings. When a friend was visiting from Germany, I wanted to make her feel at home. So I looked through a few old cookbooks and found a variation on a traditional yeasted coffee cake which called for the "cake" to be flattened and placed on a board before baking. This gave me the idea for this recipe. My friend and I enjoyed this cake for several days with our afternoon tea.

FOR THE DOUGH

9.5 ounces/269 grams (1 cup) room temperature whole milk (70°F to 78°F)

2.38 ounces/67 grams (3 teaspoons) unsalted butter

.48 ounce/13 grams (5 teaspoons) pure vanilla extract

17.83 ounces/505 grams (4 cups) unbleached all-purpose flour

.2 ounce/6 grams (2 teaspoons) instant yeast

2.38 ounces/67 grams (⅓ cup) sugar

.08 ounce/2.5 grams (½ teaspoon) fine sea salt or kosher salt

2 large eggs

FOR THE TOPPING

8 ounces/200 grams (1 cup) unsalted butter

3.52 ounces/100 grams (½ cup) sugar

.35 ounce/10 grams (1 teaspoon) pure vanilla extract

.5 ounce/25 grams (3 teaspoons) honey

1.5 ounces/75 grams (3 tablespoons) heavy cream

7.05 ounces/200 grams (2 cups) slivered almonds

I. **Make the dough:** Combine the milk and butter in a small pot and heat, stirring, until the butter is melted. Remove from the heat and stir in the vanilla. Set aside to cool to warm.

2. Combine the flour, yeast, sugar, and salt in the bowl of a standing mixer fitted with a dough hook. Add the eggs and milk mixture and give the ingredients a few turns with a rubber spatula until a rough dough forms. Knead on medium speed until the dough is smooth, 5 to 7 minutes. Cover the bowl with plastic wrap and let it stand until it has doubled in volume, about 1½ hours.

3. **Make the topping:** Combine the butter, sugar, vanilla, honey, and cream in a small saucepan. Heat over medium-high heat, stirring constantly, until the mixture comes to a boil. Turn down the heat to a simmer and stir in the almonds all at once. Remove the pot from the heat and allow the mixture to cool completely, stirring occasionally.

4. Grease a rimmed baking sheet measuring 18 by 13 inches with butter. Turn the dough onto a lightly floured countertop and knead briefly with floured hands. Roll the dough to fit the baking sheet. Spread the topping evenly over the dough. Cover the baking sheet with plastic wrap and let stand until puffy, about 1 hour.

5. Preheat the oven to 350°F. Uncover the dough and bake until the cake is golden brown and the topping is bubbling, 20 to 25 minutes. Cool the cake completely in the pan, then cut in half and use a large metal spatula to lift each half from the pan to cut and serve. Yeasted Coffee Cake with Simple Almond Topping will keep at room temperature in an airtight container for up to 2 days. For longer storage, freeze in a zipper-lock plastic bag for up to 1 month. To defrost, place on the countertop for 15 to 30 minutes, and reheat in the oven at 350°F for 5 to 10 minutes before serving.

VARIATION

YEASTED COFFEE CAKE WITH FANCY PECAN TOPPING

For a cake with fancy pecan topping, combine 1 cup of unsalted butter, ½ cup of sugar, 3 tablespoons of buttermilk, 1 tablespoon of pure maple syrup, and 1 teaspoon of bourbon (or vanilla extract—your choice) in a pot, boil as directed, and then stir in 7 ounces of pecan pieces all at once instead of the almonds. Cool, stirring, as directed, spread it on top of your cake, and bake.

CHOCOLATE BABKA

Babka is an Old World Jewish favorite that has become an almost mythical bakery item because it is so difficult to find these days. My grandmother was a great baker who regularly turned out rugelach, mandelbrot, macaroons, and honey cake. She made a fabulous chocolate babka that I remember with a mixture of nostalgia and regret, since I enjoyed it so much but never asked her to teach me how to make it. When I finally got around to coming up with my own babka recipe, I tried to make it just as wonderfully chocolatey and crumbly as hers. Best-quality European chocolate is essential (I use Callebaut). Babka is often made with cream cheese, but I like mascarpone for the hint of nutty flavor that it gives to the dough. I never have trouble coming up with uses for the leftover mascarpone (see page 126 for some ideas), but you may use regular cream cheese in its place if it's more convenient.

Shaping the babka takes several steps. First you fill the dough, and then you roll it into a log. Next you fold the log, and then you twist it, which gives the cake its interesting interior folds. While experimenting, I wished I could have asked my grandmother how she did this, but I think she'd approve of the end result.

5.77 ounces/163 grams (⅔ cup) room temperature milk (70°F to 78°F)

.72 ounce/20 grams (2 tablespoons) mascarpone cheese

7.2 ounces/204 grams (1 cup) sugar

2 large eggs

2 large egg yolks

.14 ounce/4 grams (1 teaspoon) pure vanilla extract

.08 ounce/2.5 grams (½ teaspoon) fine sea salt or kosher salt

20 ounces/570 grams (4 cups) unbleached all-purpose flour

.3 ounce/9 grams (1 tablespoon) instant yeast

5 ounces/143 grams (1¼ sticks) unsalted butter, softened and cut into bits

8 ounces/208 grams bittersweet chocolate, finely chopped

1 ounce/30 grams (2 tablespoons) heavy cream

1. Combine the milk, mascarpone cheese, ½ cup of the sugar, eggs, 1 of the egg yolks, vanilla, and salt in the bowl of a standing mixer. Stir with a rubber spatula to combine. Add the flour and yeast and stir a few times until a rough dough forms. Mix on low speed for a few minutes with the dough hook.

2. With the mixer running, add the butter, 1 piece at a time, until it is all incorporated. Turn the mixer to medium speed and knead until it comes together in a sticky but cohesive mass, 4 to 5 minutes.

3. Scrape the dough into an oiled bowl or dough-rising container and cover with plastic wrap. Refrigerate overnight, 8 to 12 hours.

4. Grease a 9 by 5-inch loaf pan. Combine the chocolate and the remaining ½ cup sugar in a medium bowl.

5. Deflate the dough by gently pressing down on it with your palms. Turn it onto a lightly floured countertop and roll it into a rough 16 by 8-inch rectangle, with the long side facing you.

6. Sprinkle the chocolate and sugar mixture over the dough. Starting with the long side closest to you, roll the dough into a snug log. Pinch the outside edges to seal.

7. Fold the log in half and twist it once in the center (giving it a shape like an awareness ribbon). Gently place the folded and twisted dough into the prepared pan. Lightly drape with plastic wrap and let rise until increased in volume by 50 percent, 1 to 2 hours (alternatively, refrigerate the dough overnight and bring to room temperature before letting it rise and baking it).

8. Preheat the oven to 350°F. Lightly beat the cream and the remaining egg yolk together in a small bowl. Brush the top of the babka with the egg wash. Bake until the top of the babka is deep golden brown and baked through, about 40 minutes. Overturn the loaf onto a wire rack, and re-invert. Let cool completely before slicing and serving. Chocolate Babka will keep at room temperature in an airtight container for up to 3 days. For longer storage, wrap in plastic wrap and then aluminum foil for up to 1 month. To defrost, place on the countertop for several hours, and reheat in the oven at 350°F for 10 minutes before serving.

USING LEFTOVER MASCARPONE

A container of mascarpone cheese in the refrigerator begs to be used in all kinds of simple dishes.

• Stir mascarpone into leftover tapenade, pesto, or baba ghanoush and serve as a dip with raw vegetables.

• Stir mascarpone into just-cooked soft polenta for the creamiest version of this dish.

• Dollop onto bowls of puréed vegetable soups—tomato, butternut squash, or broccoli—for a touch of luxurious richness.

• Whisk together ½ cup of mascarpone, ¼ cup of heavy cream, 1 cup of grated Parmesan cheese, and ½ cup of a finely chopped mixture of fresh basil, parsley, oregano, and chives in a small bowl and stir into hot cooked pasta, adding some cooking water to moisten the dish as necessary.

• Mix some mascarpone with some sugar and a little brandy or vanilla and serve alongside fresh berries or sliced pears.

• Spread sweetened mascarpone on toasted country bread, top with sliced peaches, sprinkle with cinnamon sugar, and broil briefly to caramelize the sugar.

• Fold some mascarpone into sweetened whipped cream when filling fruit shortcakes (Angel Biscuits, page 54, are great for this purpose).

• Whip together equal amounts of Nutella® and mascarpone, fill a prebaked tart shell, and top with chopped pistachio nuts and/or fresh raspberries.

CARAMEL MONKEY BREAD

Gooey caramel poured into the bottom of the pan creates just enough stickiness to hold together the nut-and-sugar-coated balls of sweet dough. The result is a pull-apart treat that is fun and festive to eat. I was expecting a crowd to gather when I offered Caramel Monkey Bread to my staff. The aroma alone was enough to draw people from near and far. Maybe because I had heard my son refer to the recipe as "monkey brains," I wasn't expecting it to be so beautiful. But it was. It is hard to resist getting your fingers seriously sticky as soon as you see it in its glossy, bumpy glory.

As a bonus, you'll wind up with more caramel than you'll need. Store it in an airtight container in the refrigerator for up to 2 weeks, and gently reheat it in a small saucepan when you want to dress up some ice cream.

FOR THE DOUGH

17.64 ounces/500 grams (4 cups) unbleached all-purpose flour

2.16 ounces/61 grams (⅓ cup) granulated sugar

.23 ounce/7.5 grams (2½ teaspoons) instant yeast

.2 ounce/6 grams (1¼ teaspoons) fine sea salt or kosher salt

7.9 ounces/245 grams (1 cup) room temperature milk (70°F to 78°F)

2.55 ounces/72 grams (⅓ cup) room temperature water (70°F to 78°F)

1.21 ounces/34 grams (2½ tablespoons) unsalted butter, softened

1 large egg

FOR THE COATING

4 ounces/113 grams (1 stick) unsalted butter, melted and cooled

5.82 ounces/165 grams (¾ cup) packed light brown sugar

1.90 ounces/54 grams (½ cup) finely chopped pecans

.25 ounce/7 grams (2 teaspoons) ground cinnamon

FOR THE CARAMEL

14.11 ounces/400 grams (2 cups) granulated sugar

1.29 ounces/36 grams (¼ cup) water

2 ounces/59 grams (¼ cup) heavy cream

1. **Make the dough:** Grease the bottom and sides of an 8-inch springform pan. Combine the flour, granulated sugar, yeast, and salt in the bowl of a standing mixer fitted with the dough hook. Add the milk, water, butter, and egg. Give the mixture a few turns with a rubber spatula to moisten all of the ingredients, and then mix on medium speed until smooth and shiny, about 2 minutes. Transfer the dough to a lightly oiled bowl or dough-rising container, cover the bowl with plastic wrap, and let stand at room temperature until it has doubled in volume, 1½ to 2 hours.

2. **Make the coating:** Place the melted butter in a bowl and combine the brown sugar, nuts, and cinnamon in another bowl. Set aside.

3. **Make the caramel:** Combine the sugar and water in a deep, heavy pot. Cook over medium heat, stirring, until the sugar is dissolved. Increase the heat to medium-high and bring to a boil, occasionally brushing down the sides of the pan with a wet pastry brush to prevent the sugar from crystallizing (don't worry if your sugar does crystallize—some crunchy bits in the bread won't be noticeable). Boil the syrup without stirring until it turns an amber color, 5 to 7 minutes, swirling the pan occasionally for even cooking.

4. Remove the syrup from the heat and stir in the cream with a long-handled wooden spoon. The mixture will bubble up (thus the need for the deep pot and the long-handled spoon). Keep stirring until the caramel is smooth. Pour a thin layer of the hot caramel into the greased springform pan so that it coats the bottom of the pan. (Let the leftover caramel cool, and then refrigerate for up to 2 weeks in an airtight container; warm the caramel in a microwave oven or on top of the stove.)

5. **Assemble the bread:** Turn the dough out onto a lightly floured countertop and cut into ½-inch pieces. Dip the balls in the melted butter and then roll in the cinnamon-sugar-nut mixture. Place the balls in the prepared pan. You will have 2 layers and a few extras to place on top. Cover the cake with plastic wrap and let rise until doubled in volume, about 1 hour.

6. Preheat the oven to 350°F. Bake until deep brown and bubbling, 35 to 40 minutes. Transfer the pan to a wire rack and let cool for 15 minutes. Then run a sharp paring knife around the perimeter of the bread, release the sides of the springform pan, and let cool for another 20 minutes on the rack. Serve warm. Caramel Monkey Bread is best served on the day it is baked.

....

VARIATION

....

GARLIC AND SCALLION MONKEY BREAD

MAKES ONE 8-INCH-ROUND

As soon as we polished off the sweet version, everyone at Bread Alone started to imagine how we might make a savory version of monkey bread. Dough balls bathed in a mixture of butter, olive oil, and garlic and seasoned with chopped scallions and Parmesan cheese was the natural way to go, and it proved just as irresistible as the sweet version.

FOR THE DOUGH

17.64 ounces/500 grams (4 cups) unbleached all-purpose flour

2.16 ounces/61 grams (⅓ cup) sugar

.23 ounce/7.5 grams (2¼ teaspoons) instant yeast

.2 ounce/6 grams (1¼ teaspoons) fine sea salt or kosher salt

7.9 ounces/245 grams (1 cup) room temperature milk (70°F to 78°F)

2.55 ounces/72 grams (⅓ cup) room temperature water (70°F to 78°F)

1.21 ounces/34 grams (2½ tablespoons) unsalted butter, softened

1 large egg

FOR THE COATING

2.5 ounces/67 grams (5 tablespoons) unsalted butter, melted and cooled

1.34 ounces/38 grams (3 tablespoons) olive oil

1 medium head garlic, cloves finely chopped

½ bunch scallions, white and green parts, finely chopped

.6 ounce/17 grams (½ cup) grated Parmesan cheese

1. **Make the dough:** Grease the bottom and sides of an 8-inch springform pan. Combine the flour, sugar, yeast, and salt in the bowl of a standing mixer fitted with the dough hook. Add the milk, water, butter, and egg. Give the mixture a few turns with a rubber spatula to moisten all of the ingredients, and then mix on medium speed until smooth and shiny, about 2 minutes. Transfer the dough to a lightly oiled bowl or dough-rising container, cover the bowl with plastic wrap, and let stand at room temperature until it has doubled in volume, 1½ to 2 hours.

2. **Make the coating:** Combine the melted butter and olive oil in a medium bowl. Combine the garlic and half of the scallions in another bowl.

3. **Assemble the bread:** Turn the dough out onto a lightly floured countertop and cut into ½-inch pieces. Dip the balls in the butter and oil mixture, 1 at a time, and place them in the prepared pan. When you have a single layer of dough balls, sprinkle with two-thirds of the garlic-scallion mixture. Roll the remaining dough balls in the butter and oil, arrange in the pan, and sprinkle with the remaining one-third of the garlic and scallions, tucking the scallion pieces into the crevasses between the balls. Cover the bread with plastic wrap and let rise until doubled in volume, about 1 hour.

4. Preheat the oven to 350°F. Bake until just brown, 30 to 35 minutes. Sprinkle the cheese over the bread and continue to bake until the cheese has melted, another 5 minutes. Transfer the pan to a wire rack and let cool for 15 minutes. Then run a sharp paring knife around the perimeter of the bread, release the sides of the springform pan, and let cool for another 20 minutes on the rack. Serve warm. Garlic and Scallion Monkey Bread is best served on the day it's baked.

EQUIVALENCY CHARTS

OVEN TEMPERATURES

Gas Mark	°F	°C
½	250	120
1	275	140
2	300	150
3	325	165
4	350	180
5	375	190
6	400	200
7	425	220
8	450	230
9	475	240
10	500	260
Broil	550	290

LIQUID/DRY MEASURES

U.S.	Metric
¼ teaspoon	1.25 milliliters
½ teaspoon	2.5 milliliters
1 teaspoon	5 milliliters
1 tablespoon (3 teaspoons)	15 milliliters
1 fluid ounce (2 tablespoons)	30 milliliters
¼ cup	60 milliliters
⅓ cup	80 milliliters
½ cup	120 milliliters
1 cup	240 milliliters
1 pint (2 cups)	480 milliliters
1 quart (4 cups; 32 ounces)	960 milliliters
1 gallon (4 quarts)	3.84 liters
1 ounce (by weight)	28 grams
1 pound	454 grams
2.2 pounds	1 kilogram

GLOSSARY OF BAKING TERMS

Baguette: A long, thin loaf of French bread. In France, there are actually guidelines set down by French law that define its shape and size, which should be 5 to 6 centimeters in diameter and up to 1 meter in length, with a typical weight of 250 grams. Home bakers will have difficulty crafting very long baguettes, which won't fit in the typical home oven, but in the United States our standards for bread are less strict than they are in France!

Biga: An Italian-style yeasted pre-ferment. A *biga* usually has a stiff, dough-like consistency.

Bran: The outermost layer of the wheat kernel. Bran is edible but contains minerals and indigestible cellulose, which adds to a bread's fiber and mineral content.

Bromate: A chemical additive that hastens the aging process of flour, making it ready for baking earlier than natural aging would.

Crumb: The interior of the bread. Crumb can be loose and large (typical of artisan breads raised with sourdough) or tight and small (softer white breads and many whole grain breads have a tighter crumb structure).

Direct dough: Another term for the straight-dough method of mixing dough in one stage rather than in two.

Elasticity: A dough's ability to bounce back when stretched. Glutenin, one of the gluten-forming proteins in wheat flour (along with gliadin), is responsible for a dough's elasticity.

Fermentation: The process by which yeast breaks down flour's starches, producing carbon dioxide and alcohol as by-products.

Folding: A technique used to strengthen the gluten in a dough without over-kneading it, by lifting it from the dough-rising container and replacing it back down midway through fermentation.

Fresh yeast: Commercial yeast that hasn't been fully dried, but is packaged instead in moist cakes. Fresh yeast (also known as compressed yeast) has a much shorter shelf life than dried yeast (it loses potency a few weeks after it is packaged). It used to be popular with professional bakers, who go through a lot more yeast than home bakers, but has been supplanted by longer-lasting dried yeast.

Gluten: The protein web formed when proteins in wheat flour link together as a dough is formed and kneaded. Gluten gives

dough its structure, expanding as the gases produced during fermentation expand, so that the dough rises.

Hydration: The amount of water relative to flour in bread dough.

Instant yeast: Commercial dried yeast that does not require rehydration before being mixed into dough. Choose instant yeast for bread-machine baking, where all of the ingredients are simply added to the bread pan with no opportunity for hydrating the yeast ahead of time.

Kneading: The vigorous working of the dough, either by hand or machine, to distribute the dough's ingredients evenly and to develop gluten structure.

Levain: The French term for a sourdough starter, *levain* is usually stiff and dough-like, but the term can also refer to a liquid sourdough.

Oven spring: The rapid rise of bread dough during the first few minutes of baking.

Pre-ferment: A percentage of a dough's flour, water, and yeast mixed together at least several hours and up to several days before the dough is mixed and then added to the dough to "age" it and give it more flavor without the risk of over-fermenting it.

Proofing: The period of bread dough's second rise, after bulk fermentation and shaping.

Retarding: Refrigerating the dough either before or after it is shaped to slow down fermentation.

Sourdough bread: Bread raised with wild as opposed to commercially raised and packaged yeast.

Sourdough starter: Wild yeast, cultivated in a mixture of flour and water, and used instead of or along with commercial yeast to raise bread.

Sponge: The English term for a wet pre-ferment made with flour, water, and commercial yeast.

Straight dough: A bread dough mixed in one step, with no pre-ferment or sourdough starter, in which commercial yeast is added directly to the dough.

Whole wheat: Whole wheat flour contains the entire milled wheat kernel—germ, bran, and endosperm—as opposed to white wheat flour, which consists primarily of starchy endosperm.

Yeast: Single-celled microorganisms that produce carbon dioxide (along with alcohol) as they feed on starches in bread dough, causing the dough to rise as it ferments and bakes.

RESOURCES

You can make any of the recipes in this book with ingredients and equipment found at your local supermarket, natural foods store, and cookware shop. But it is fun and interesting to investigate the variety of organic flours, freshly ground spices, and professional-quality cake rings available with the click of a mouse. The following are some of my favorite sources when I want to shop from home.

Breadtopia, www.breadtopia.com
This online store sells every imaginable piece of bread-baking equipment, including baker's peels, digital scales, and thermometers. This is also the place to buy SAF instant yeast, my preferred brand, in bulk.

Chef's Warehouse®, www.chefswarehouse.com
This is the place to go for 4-pound cans of Bazzini® nuts and seeds, bulk Valrhona chocolate, unusual honeys and jams, and chestnut purée.

Cooking.com®, www.cooking.com
This online cookware store runs frequent specials on pricey items such as KitchenAid stand mixers and offers great deals on baking stone and peel sets. Since they sell all kinds of pots and pans, they always stock the cast-iron pans and griddles that I use to create steam in the oven and to bake flatbreads on top of my stove.

Giusto's Vita-Grain Flours®, www.guistos.com
Based in San Francisco, Giusto's has long been the choice of professional artisan bakers on the West Coast. Recently, the company has begun to package its carefully milled flours in smaller quantities for home bakers. So if you want to use the same flour that is used at Berkeley's famed Acme Bread Company, visit this site.

King Arthur Flour Company, www.kingarthurflour.com
King Arthur sells a great variety of high-quality flours and grains, including the organic all-purpose flour that I used to test many of the recipes in this book. You can also find Italian-style *tipo oo* flour and many other specialty milled flours that are difficult to find anywhere else. More than a flour source, it is a one-stop shop for the bread baker, stocking every ingredient and piece of equipment that you might need, including malt powder, pearl sugar, SAF yeast, fleur de sel, rose water and orange blossom water, chocolate, hand-crank pasta machines, cake rings, and precut sheets of parchment paper in bulk.

Lehman's*, www.lehmans.com
For a cast iron waffle iron that sits right on the stove.

Nuts Online®, www.nutsonline.com
This online retailer sells very fresh nuts and seeds in large, but not ridiculously large, quantities. They have a wide selection of organic nuts, seeds, and dried fruits at very fair prices for bakers committed to using 100 percent organic ingredients in their breads.

Penzeys Spices®, www.penzeys.com
For freshly ground and hard-to-find spices, this is the place to go. Order from an impressive menu of cinnamons and chili powders. This is also the place to find the Middle Eastern spice mix za'atar or the individual spices to mix your own.

Salt Traders, www.salttraders.com
Purveyors of sea salts and other fine salts from around the world; many are sold in bulk for economy and convenience.

SaltWorks®, www.saltworks.us/
This Seattle-based company provides fine sea salt to restaurants and gourmet markets as well as sells smaller quantities to retail customers online.

Williams-Sonoma, www.williams-sonoma.com
This well-known chain sells top-quality appliances such as KitchenAid mixers and All-Clad waffle irons, as well as professional-quality baking sheets and nonstick Gold-touch loaf and cake pans.

INDEX

Numbers in **bold** indicate pages with illustrations

A
Almonds
  Yeasted Coffee Cake with Simple Almond Topping, 121–22
Angel Biscuits, 10, 50, 54–55
Anise seeds
  Cherry Tomato–Anise *Schiacciata*, 84
Apple cider
  Cider Doughnuts, 5, 108–10, **110**
Apricots and apricot jam
  Quick Apricot–Chocolate Chip Spirals, 40
  Whole Wheat Challah with Apricots, 71–72, 73
Artisan bread recipes and simple baking, 4–5
Artistry, leading lives of, 29

B
Babka, 97
  Chocolate Babka, 20, 98, 123–25, **124**
Bagels, 5, 25
  Authentic Bagels, 45–47, 85
Baking stones, 10, 17, 51
Banana Doughnuts with Maple-Walnut Glaze, 111–13
Beef stew, 51
Beignets
  Stone Fruit Beignets, 114–16, **117**
Bialys, 24, 25
  Boiceville Bialys, 41–44, **42**, 85
Biga, 63, 64, 65, 66, 67
Biscuits
  Angel Biscuits, 10, 50, 54–55
Bowls, mixing, 19
Bran
  Ciabatta with Bran, 65
Bread Alone, 4, 33, 41, 65, 97, 111
Bread Alone (Leader), 3
Bread and treats
  equipment for baking, 14, 17–20, 134
  freezing, 50, 101
  ingredients, 6, 10–11, 13–14, 98, 134
  internal temperatures, 19–20
  simple baking, 4–5, 24
  suggestions for making, 6, 9–10
  time needed for, 4, 5, 65
Bread basket, ideal, 49–50

Bread flour, 25, 33
Bread shaping
  pan loaf, 40
  rounds, 44
Bread sticks
  Crisp Bread Sticks, **60**, 61–62
  Extra-Crisp Bread Sticks, 62
  Italian bread sticks, 5, 50, 61
  pasta machine for forming, 5, 19, 50, 61
  simple baking, 4–5
Breakfast breads, 23–25
  Authentic Bagels, 45–47, 85
  Boiceville Bialys, 41–44, **42**, 85
  Brioche Muffins, 25, 33–36, **34**, **36**
  Chestnut Brioche Muffins, 36
  Cinnamon-Cardamom Brioche Muffins, 36
  Crumpets, **30**, 31–32
  Fig Brioche Muffins, 36
  "Luxury" English Muffins, 26–28, **27**, 44
  Quick Apricot–Chocolate Chip Spirals, 40
  Quick Chestnut Cinnamon Sugar Spirals, 37–40, **38**
  Quick Cocoa-Mascarpone Spirals, 40
Brioche
  Brioche Muffins, 25, 33–36, **34**, **36**
  Quick Apricot–Chocolate Chip Spirals, 40
  Quick Chestnut Cinnamon Sugar Spirals, 37–40, **38**
  Quick Cocoa-Mascarpone Spirals, 40
  traditional shaping, 33, 37
Butter, 13
Buttermilk, 13

C
Cake rings, 18
Caramel Monkey Bread, 98, 127–28, **129**
Challah
  Whole Wheat Challah with Apricots, 71–72, **73**
  Whole Wheat Challah with Green Olives, 73
Cheese, 13
  Fontina *Bomboloni*, 44, 117–18, **119**
  Ham-and-Cheese-Filled Crescent Rolls, 58–59
  See also Mascarpone cheese
Chestnut purée, 37
  Chestnut Brioche Muffins, 36
  Quick Chestnut Cinnamon

Sugar Spirals, 37–40, **38**
Chicken
  Mousakhan (Palestinian Chicken and Onions), 94–95
Chili-Dusted Navajo Fry Bread, 70
Chocolate, 13
  Chocolate Babka, 20, 98, 123–25, **124**
  Quick Apricot–Chocolate Chip Spirals, 40
  Quick Cocoa-Mascarpone Spirals, 40
Ciabatta
  Ciabatta Rolls, 20, 63–65, 85
  Ciabatta with Bran, 65
  Grilled Savory of Sweet *Ciabatta*, 66–67
  internal temperature, 20
  pre-ferment, 10
  Seven-Seed *Ciabatta* Rolls, 65
  water in, 6
Cinnamon
  Cinnamon-Cardamom Brioche Muffins, 36
  fermentation and, 99
  Quick Chestnut Cinnamon Sugar Spirals, 37–40, **38**
Coffee cake, 97, 98
  Yeasted Coffee Cake with Fancy Pecan Topping, 122
  Yeasted Coffee Cake with Simple Almond Topping, 121–22
Cooling racks, 20
Cornmeal, 14, 24
Crumpets, 24, **30**, 31–32

D
Doughnut Plant, 41
Doughnuts, 97, 98
  Banana Doughnuts with Maple-Walnut Glaze, 111–13
  Cider Doughnuts, 5, 108–10, **110**
  Fontina *Bomboloni*, 44, 117–18, **119**
  Glazed Cider Doughnuts, 110
  Jelly-Filled Berliners, 98, **103**, 103–4, **105**
  simple baking, 4–5

E
Eggs, 14
  Mana'eesh with Baked Eggs, 92–93
English muffin rings, 18, 26, 29
English muffins, 24
  "Luxury" English Muffins, 26–28, **27**, 44

Equipment for baking, 14, 17–20, 134
Equivalency charts, 132

F
Figs
  Fig Brioche Muffins, 36
  Fig Jam, 107
Flatbreads, 75–77
  Cherry Tomato–Anise *Schiacciata*, 84
  Grape *Schiacciata*, 5, 82–84, **83**, 85
  Mana'eesh, 75, 76, 77, 89–93
  Mana'eesh with Baked Eggs, 92–93
  Pizza Dough for Grilling, 78–81, **79**, 85
  Pizza Dough with Honey and Wine, 80–81
  Rosemary-Walnut *Schiacciata*, 84
  Savory Yeasted Tart with Onion Confit and Olives, 86–88
Flax seeds
  Whole Wheat and Flax Seed Yeasted Waffles, 102
Flour
  gluten and, 9, 33
  resources, 134
  types of, 10–11, 78
  weighing, 6
Freezing bread and treats, 50, 101
Fried bread
  Chili-Dusted Navajo Fry Bread, 70
  Navajo Fry Bread, 44, 68–70, **69**
Fruit, dried, 14

G
Garlic and Scallion Monkey Bread, 130–31
Glossary, 133
Gluten, 9, 11, 33
Grape *Schiacciata*, 5, 82–84, **83**, 85
Grilled breads
  Grilled Savory of Sweet *Ciabatta*, 66–67
  Pizza Dough for Grilling, 78–81, **79**, 85
  Pizza Dough with Honey and Wine, 80–81

H
Ham-and-Cheese-Filled Crescent Rolls, 58–59

Honey
Pizza Dough with Honey and
Wine, 80–81

I
Ingredients, 6, 10–11, 13–14,
98, 134
Italian breads
biga, 63, 64, 65, 66, 67
water in, 6
See also Ciabatta
Italian bread sticks, 5, 50, 61

J
Jams and preserves, 103, 106
Fig Jam, 107
Peach and Rosemary Jam, 107
Strawberry Jam, 106
Juice cans, 29

K
Kneading, 9, 85
Knives, 19
Kossar's Bialys, 25, 41

L
Laurel's Kitchen (Robertson),
26, 29
Leader, Liv, 75, 76, 89, 94
Local Breads (Leader), 3

M
Malt powder, 14, 25, 45
Authentic Bagels, 45–47, 85
Mana'eesh, 75, 76, 77, 89–93
Maple syrup
Banana Doughnuts with
Maple-Walnut Glaze, 111–13
Mascarpone cheese
Chocolate Babka, 20, 98,
123–25, **124**
leftover, using, 126
Quick Cocoa-Mascarpone
Spirals, 40
Mastman's Kosher
Delicatessen, 25
Measuring cups and spoons,
18–19
Milk, 14
Mixers, 9, 18, 85, 134
Monkey bread
Caramel Monkey Bread, 98,
127–28, **129**
Garlic and Scallion Monkey
Bread, 130–31
Mousakhan (Palestinian
Chicken and Onions), 94–95
Muffin tin, 19

N
Navajo Fry Bread, 44, 68–70, **69**
Nuts and seeds, 14, 134
See also specific Types

O
Oil, olive, 14
Oil, vegetable, 14
Olives
Savory Yeasted Tart with
Onion Confit and Olives,
86–88
Whole Wheat Challah with
Green Olives, 73
Onions
Boiceville Bialys, 41–44, **42**
Mousakhan (Palestinian
Chicken and Onions), 94–95
Savory Yeasted Tart with
Onion Confit and Olives,
86–88
Organic ingredients, 6, 98
Oven thermometers, 20

P
Pancakes, 98
Yeasted Pancakes, 5, 98,
99–100
Pans
baking, 17
cake, 17
cast-iron, 17–18
loaf, 18, 29
resources, 134
Parchment paper, 19
Parker House Rolls, 4–5, 49
Lightly Shaped Parker House
Rolls, 50, 51–52, **53**
Pasta machine, 5, 19, 50, 61
Pastry brush, 19
Peaches
Peach and Rosemary Jam, 107
Stone Fruit Beignets, 114–16,
117
Pearl sugar, 33
Pecans
Yeasted Coffee Cake with
Fancy Pecan Topping, 122
Pizza
flour for, 78
grilled, 66, 76, 77
Pizza Dough for Grilling,
78–81, **79**, 85
Pizza Dough with Honey and
Wine, 80–81
Pizza cutter, 19
Plastic wrap, 19
Practicing a recipe, 10
Pre-ferment, 9–10, 45, 51

Processed foods, 98
Proofing dough, 10

R
Resources, 134
Rolling pins, 19
Rolls
Ciabatta Rolls, 20, 63–65, 85
Ciabatta with Bran, 65
Ham-and-Cheese-Filled
Crescent Rolls, 58–59
Lightly Shaped Parker House
Rolls, 50, 51–52, **53**
Parker House Rolls, 4–5, 49
Seven-Seed *Ciabatta* Rolls, 65
Rosemary
Peach and Rosemary Jam, 107
Rosemary-Walnut
Schiacciata, 84

S
Salt, 13, 66, 134
Sandwiches, filling ideas for, 63
Scale, 6, 18
Schiacciata, 85
Cherry Tomato–Anise
Schiacciata, 84
Grape *Schiacciata*, 5, 82–84,
83
Rosemary-Walnut
Schiacciata, 84
Seeds and nuts, 14, 134
Seven-Seed *Ciabatta* Rolls, 65
See also specific Types
Sesame seeds
Za'atar, 91
Shrimp Salad, 57
Simple baking, 4–5, 24
Sourdough breads
books about, 3–4
characteristics of, 65
learning to bake, 3
time needed for, 4, 65
Spatulas, 19
Starters
care and feeding of, 4
wild yeast starter, 4
Stone Fruit Beignets, 114–16, **117**
Strawberry Jam, 106
Sumac
Mana'eesh with Baked Eggs,
92–93
Mousakhan (Palestinian
Chicken and Onions), 94–95
Za'atar, 91

T
Temperature
of ingredients, 9

in the kitchen, 6
for rising, 9
thermometers, 19–20
Thermometers, 19–20
Tomatoes
Cherry Tomato–Anise
Schiacciata, 84
Marinara Dipping Sauce, 120
Tuna cans, 26, 29

U
Union Square Greenmarket, 41

V
Vegetables, roasted, 51

W
Waffle iron, 20, 101, 134
Waffles, 98
Whole Wheat and Flax Seed
Yeasted Waffles, 102
Yeast-Raised Waffles, 101–2
Walnuts
Banana Doughnuts with
Maple-Walnut Glaze, 111–13
Rosemary-Walnut
Schiacciata, 84
Water, 6, 11
Whole wheat breads and treats
Whole Wheat and Flax Seed
Yeasted Waffles, 102
Whole Wheat Challah with
Apricots, 71–72, **73**
Whole Wheat Challah with
Green Olives, 73
Whole wheat flour, 11
Wine
Pizza Dough with Honey and
Wine, 80–81

Y
Yeast
commercial yeast, recipes
for, 4
resources, 134
types of, 11, 13
wild yeast starter, 4
Yeasted treats, 97–98

Z
Za'atar, 91